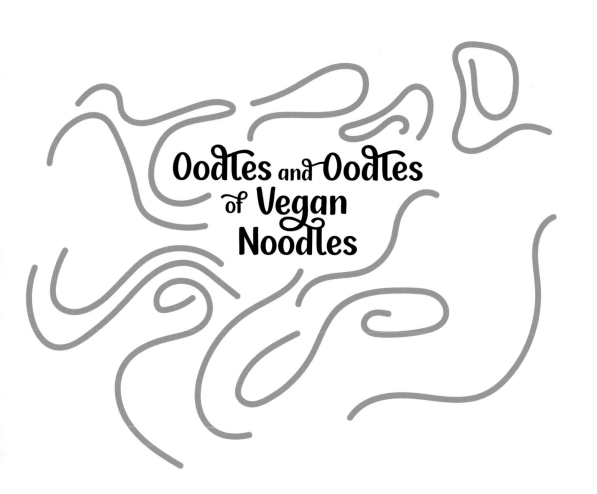

Oodles and Oodles of Vegan Noodles

Oodles and Oodles of Vegan Noodles

SOBA, RAMEN, UDON & MORE

CHEYNESE KHACHAME

THE EXPERIMENT

NEW YORK

Contents

More Noodle Recipes

CREAMY
COCONUT-CURRY
RAMEN
(PAGE 95)

Introduction

My love of cooking came naturally once I became vegan. I like to veganize all kinds of recipes, and I hope that I can inspire others, vegan or not, to try them. I'm drawn to many different cuisines, but I must admit I have a weakness for Asian food (Japanese, Korean, Chinese, Thai, Vietnamese, and Laotian, mainly). This preference led me to fall in love with noodles.

When I went vegan, I never imagined I would have so many appetizing choices. Now I want to share these recipes with as large an audience as possible, beyond my already loyal TikTok and Instagram fans.

We like to eat food that looks appetizing, and this is why—with joy and good cheer—I like to perfect the presentation, adding simple garnishes to each dish. Our mental and physical health is affected by what we eat, and with these recipes I hope to impart how much gustatory pleasure you can get from these delectable and 100 percent vegan dishes.

In this book I share my passion, and I hope this will encourage you to try my recipes and inspire you to give vegan cooking a try!

Rice Noodles: Used in many Asian dishes, they are an excellent staple to have on hand. Naturally gluten-free, they can be used for stir-fried noodle dishes and in soups.

Rice Vermicelli: These noodles are very thin, white as snow, and they look and feel delicate.

Pantry Staples

NOODLES

Soba (Buckwheat Noodles): These Japanese noodles are full of protein and fiber. Their delicious, nutty flavor comes from their strong, earthy buckwheat base.

Somen: These Japanese wheat flour noodles are enriched with oil to make them thin and delicate. They're used in the same way as soba noodles but have a more sophisticated flavor.

Ramen: This is a traditional Japanese noodle, originally imported from China. Rippled and yellow in color, they are made from wheat flour, baking soda, and food coloring.

Tteok Bokki: These Korean rice cakes are like very thick, short, cylindrical noodles. They cook up chewy and filling.

Somyeon Noodles: A Korean version of wheat flour–based somen noodles.

Mung Bean Noodles: These transparent noodles ("cellophane noodles") are made from mung bean starch, and are sold dried. They're frequently used in Vietnamese summer rolls.

Chinese Wheat Noodles: Very yellow in color from food coloring, these noodles are ideal for stews, soups, and stir-fries. They're sometimes called "chow mein noodles."

Jjajangmyeon Noodles: These thick, chewy wheat flour noodles are usually sold frozen. Thaw before using.

Udon: Extremely popular in Japan, these thick wheat-flour noodles are available in a variety of lengths and widths. Sold dried, fresh, and frozen.

Dangmyeon (Sweet Potato Noodles): Originally from Korea, these classic noodles have a sweet potato starch base. They're sometimes referred to as "glass noodles."

Naengmyeon (Buckwheat and Potato Noodles): These Korean noodles are made with a combination of starches, most often a combination of buckwheat and potato starch.

Seaweeds

Kombu: This crunchy, lightly salty, and slightly sweet seaweed is particularly appreciated for its umami, the famous and delicious "fifth taste." It is used to flavor broths and sauces but is not usually eaten.

Nori: This seaweed—with its salty, iodized, and slightly herbaceous flavor—has been used in Japanese cuisine for centuries.

Wakame: This seaweed is a useful addition to salads and soups, among them the delicious and popular miso soup.

KOMBU

NORI

WAKAME

SHICHIMI TOGARASHI

Flours, Sugars, Spices

All-Purpose Flour: A classic pantry staple.

Sweet Rice Flour: Derived from sticky or glutinous rice.

Cornstarch: Helps thicken sauces. Mix with water to make a slurry, then stir into the liquid to be thickened a little at a time.

Superfine Cane or Brown Sugar: Helps counterbalance salty dishes and adds a rich caramel color. Superfine sugar dissolves more easily than regular granulated sugar in cold sauces and dressings, but granulated is fine for cooking.

Gochugaru: Korean chile available in ground or flake form, it's mildly spicy, fruity, and adds color. It's the ultimate all-purpose spice.

Freshly Ground Black Pepper: Essential for seasoning.

Sichuan Pepper: This pepper—which is not really pepper, but the berry of the prickly ash—is crucial to the Chinese pantry.

Shichimi Togarashi: A Japanese blend of seven (shichimi) spices including red pepper. It's great for adding zip to plain noodles.

Nuts, Seeds

Peanuts: Often used as a garnish.

Peanut Butter: Often used in sauces and marinades.

Sesame Seeds: White or sometimes black, they are a flavorful garnish. White sesame seeds may be toasted for extra flavor.

Sesame Paste (Tahini): Smooth, puréed sesame seeds. Often used with other condiments such as soy sauce and rice vinegar. Available in Middle Eastern stores. Smooth peanut butter may be substituted.

TAHINI

Asian Condiments and Ingredients

Soy Sauce: The "mother" sauce of Asian cuisine that replaces salt and adds umami to all dishes. Light soy sauce is most commonly used, but there is also thicker, slightly sweet dark soy sauce.

Toasted Sesame Oil: An aromatic oil with a slightly nutty flavor. Principally used as a garnish, it can be used in some wok-cooked dishes.

Mirin: This sweetened Asian wine is originally from Japan and is used as a condiment. It's similar to sake, but with less alcohol and a sweeter flavor.

Rice Vinegar: Derived from the fermentation of rice, it's milder and sweeter than wine vinegar. It's used in sushi rice and also works well in other dishes.

Black Vinegar: Derived from the fermentation of black sticky rice, this vinegar is specific to China and adds acidity to Chinese cooking.

Gochujang (Korean Chile Pepper Paste): This spicy Korean condiment is made from red chiles, meju (dried fermented soybeans), sweet white rice flour, and wheat.

Chunjang (Black Bean Paste): Made from salted fermented soybeans, this caramel-colored condiment is essential for making Noodles in Black Bean Sauce (page 115).

Miso: A paste made of fermented soybeans. Its salty flavor adds savoriness to a dish and can be used in place of salt. Different colors have different intensities; white is the mildest, brown is stronger, and red is the strongest.

Chile Oil: The basis for many regional Chinese cuisines, it is made by infusing chiles (and sometimes other ingredients) in hot oil.

Fish Sauce: An essential ingredient in Thai cooking as well as other Asian cuisines, it has a rich reddish-brown, translucent appearance. See page 19 for a vegan version.

Oyster Sauce: Both salty and slightly sweet, it adds a depth of flavor without drowning out other ingredients. See page 18 for a vegan version.

TOFU

MISO

Shaoxing Wine: Like soy sauce, this is an important ingredient in Chinese cooking. It has a light brown color and a delicious umami flavor. It adds depth and flavor to any dish. Check your local Asian or specialty grocery store for this wine; if you are unable to find it, feel free to substitute sherry, rice vinegar, sake, or mirin.

Tofu: Comes in several degrees of firmness—silken, soft, firm, and extra firm. Silken is ideal for blending into smoothies and desserts and adding to Japanese miso soup. Soft is best for soups and heftier stews. The firm and extra firm types keep their shape when fried or baked. Be sure to drain it well before using. For frying, it helps to press out the extra liquid first. Place the tofu between two layers of paper or kitchen towels, then place a weight, such as a can of beans, on top. Allow to sit until the towels stop absorbing moisture.

Seitan: A firm, chewy protein-rich food made from wheat gluten. Its flavor is rather neutral, so it picks up flavor from the foods and sauces with which it's cooked.

SHIITAKE MUSHROOMS

Bok Choy: The most popular vegetable in China, it has a light and slightly sweet taste and crunchy consistency. Look for small heads with green stems and leaves, not tiny baby bok choy or large heads with white stems.

Bean Sprouts: Usually grown from mung beans. It is worth seeking out fresh bean sprouts. If you must use canned, rinse and drain them well first.

Produce

Ginger: Used in everything from oils to sauces to side dishes, ginger adds a warm citrusy flavor that can enliven a dish.

Scallions, Leeks, Chives: An essential ingredient in stir-fries, they are an excellent way to add a light oniony flavor to any Asian dish.

Cilantro: Often used as a garnish.

Cucumber: Often used as a garnish, and in kimchi. English or hothouse cucumbers need no peeling; garden cucumbers sometimes have a thick skin that needs to be removed.

Daikon: A large, white Japanese radish that can be marinated, served raw in salads, or simmered in soups.

Shiitake Mushrooms: These mushrooms add a unique, earthy umami flavor. With their meaty firmness, they are often used in the place of meat. Always remove the inedible stems from fresh shiitakes before using. Dried shiitake mushrooms give a flavor lift to soups and stews. When reconstituted, they can be added to stuffings and stir-fries.

DAIKON

Utensils

Chopsticks: Used in some Asian cuisines for both cooking and eating, chopsticks especially lend themselves to handling small, bite-size foods and, of course, noodles.

Wok: An indispensable tool in Asian cooking, a wok has several advantages. Its rounded bottom allows the ingredients to cook evenly, resulting in a shorter cooking time and less need for oil, for healthier food.

Glass Preserving Jars: Useful for storing infused oils and kimchi.

SPICY OIL INFUSED
WITH GARLIC,
GOCHUGARU, AND
SESAME SEEDS
(PAGE 10)

SCALLION-
INFUSED OIL
(PAGE 11)

Basics

Spicy Oil Infused with Garlic, Gochugaru, and Sesame Seeds

This spicy and crunchy condiment—a homemade version of the popular chili crisp—is infused with garlic, gochugaru, sesame seeds, and salt. The result is a meaty, savory umami flavor, full of texture and deliciousness. This is one of my favorite condiments—I love adding it to rice, sauces, and of course noodles. For this recipe, I used gochugaru in flake form, rather than the ground version. I like to use it to add a smoky flavor without making the oil too spicy.

1. Mix the gochugaru, sesame seeds, garlic, and salt in a 16-ounce (480 ml) glass preserving jar.

2. Heat the oil in a saucepan over high heat for about 1 minute, until barely smoking. Slowly pour it into the jar. (The oil will sizzle—that's normal!) Stir to combine.

3. Allow to cool to room temperature, then cover tightly.

MAKES ABOUT 2 CUPS (500 ML)

3 tablespoons gochugaru flakes

¼ cup (35 g) sesame seeds

10 garlic cloves, minced

1 tablespoon fine salt

1¼ cups (300 ml) vegetable oil or other neutral oil

(Tip:) The oil will stay fresh for 1 month, stored in the refrigerator, tightly capped.

Scallion-Infused Oil

Scallion-Infused Oil (also referred to as "green onion oil") is indispensable in Cantonese cooking, and is amazingly easy to make. It's a great way to add a pleasing aroma and a bit of dimension to a dish, and the vibrant green color creates a nice contrast. It goes well with rice, tofu, sautéed vegetables, and noodles. This oil isn't only used in Cantonese cooking—the Vietnamese use it in banh mi and pour it over grilled eggplant and noodles. In Singapore, it is served with Hainanese chicken and rice, and in Korea it's simply added to hot rice. Don't worry when you see the amount of oil called for in this recipe, as you're not meant to use all of the oil at one time.

1. Heat the oil in a deep saucepan over medium heat. After 30 seconds, test the heat by dropping a piece of scallion into the oil. If it sizzles, the oil is ready.

2. Pour the scallions into the oil and stir, preferably with a chopstick, for 30 to 40 seconds but no longer. Remove from the heat and allow to cool to room temperature.

3. Pour the oil and scallions into a 24-ounce (700 ml) glass preserving jar. Add the salt and mix well. (Don't remove the scallions from the oil!) Cover, and store in the refrigerator.

MAKES ABOUT 3 CUPS (720 ML)

2 cups (480 ml) vegetable oil or other neutral oil

10 scallions (white and green parts), thinly sliced

1 teaspoon fine salt

Tip: The oil will stay fresh for 1 week, stored in the refrigerator, tightly capped.

Vegetable Dashi

Dashi is a Japanese broth. This basic ingredient adds authentic flavor to numerous Japanese dishes. You could say it's the key to Japanese cooking. It's used in various recipes such as miso soup, soba noodle soup, udon noodle soup, ramen noodle soup, and stir-fries. Traditional dashi is made from kombu (dried kelp, 昆布) plus fish such as niboshi (small dried anchovies) or katsuobushi (bonito flakes). The vegan recipe I'm sharing here uses kombu and dried mushrooms.

1. Combine 3⅓ cups (800 ml) water with the mushrooms and kombu in a glass bowl. (Make sure the mushrooms and kombu are fully submerged.) Cover and allow to sit in the refrigerator to infuse for a minimum of 5 hours.

2. When the dashi turns brown in color, strain it into a 1-quart (1 L) glass preserving jar and cover. (Reserve the mushrooms and kombu for another use, if desired.)

MAKES ABOUT 3⅓ CUPS (800 ML)

3 dried shiitake mushrooms, stems removed

1 piece (about 0.3 oz/10 g) kombu

Tip: **The dashi will keep, covered, for 1 week in the refrigerator.**

Soup Stock * MENTSUYU

Mentsuyu is a Japanese sauce base or soup stock used in many noodle dishes. This base, which you can find in every Japanese refrigerator, is made with only a handful of ingredients. It needs to be diluted before use, as it's a concentration of very strong flavors.

1. Add the sake, mirin, soy sauce, mushrooms, and kombu to a saucepan and bring to a boil. Turn down the heat and simmer for 5 minutes. Remove from the heat and allow to cool to room temperature.

2. Strain into a bottle with a cap or half-gallon (2 L) glass preserving jar, and cover. (Reserve the mushrooms and kombu for another use, if desired.) Store in the refrigerator.

MAKES ABOUT 1 QUART (1 L)

1 cup (240 ml) sake

2¼ cups (540 ml) mirin

2 cups (480 ml) light soy sauce

3 dried shiitake mushrooms, stems removed

2 sheets kombu

(Tips:) This mixture is very practical, as it keeps for about 1 month in the refrigerator. You can also buy it ready-made from your local Japanese grocery store.

It's important to dilute the sauce before consuming. For a dipping sauce, dilute with about 2 cups (480 ml) ice water. For a lighter taste, I recommend 2 parts ice water to 1 part mentsuyu. For example, dilute ½ cup (120 ml) premade mentsuyu with 1 cup (240 ml) ice water. You can also add it to your favorite broths and sauces to taste.

Chinese Cabbage Kimchi

The first time I ate kimchi (김치), I wasn't a fan. It took me a while to come back to it, and after my second taste, I decided to make my own. The result: I loved it! Kimchi is a vegetable (usually cabbage) that is fermented in a bright red hot pepper sauce generally composed of gochugaru, ginger, garlic, and fruit (such as Asian pear, apple, or kiwi.) Kimchi is a staple of Korean cooking; you'll find it served with every meal.

1. Chop the cabbage in half lengthwise, then slice each half in two lengthwise. Rinse the cabbage under running water. Stuff with coarse salt between each leaf. (It's very important that all of the leaves are well salted.) Place on a paper or kitchen towel and allow to sit for 2 hours, until the leaves have released their liquid have released their liquid. Rinse well to remove excess salt.

2. To make the marinade, combine the carrot, apple, scallions, garlic, onion, and ginger in a medium bowl. Stir well.

3. Mix the rice flour with 2 cups (480 ml) water in a small saucepan over medium heat until it thickens slightly but does not become a paste. Pour the rice flour mixture into the bowl with the marinade and mix well. Add the gochugaru a little at a time, mixing well. (Use more or less gochugaru according to your preference for heat.)

4. Working with one cabbage quarter at a time, cut off most of the core, keeping just enough to hold the leaves together. Gently pull back the layers of leaves, spreading the marinade generously between them as well as on the outer leaves. Fold each cabbage quarter in half along the horizontal axis, then wrap its two outermost leaves around the folded quarter. Place in a glass bowl or half-gallon (2 L) glass preserving jar. Repeat with the remaining cabbage quarters. Press down on the cabbage to release air pockets. Pour over the remaining marinade and cover the container.

5. Allow the kimchi to ferment at room temperature for 2 to 3 days in a cool kitchen spot, or half a day during hot weather. Once fermented, keep refrigerated, covered.

MAKES ABOUT 2 QUARTS (2 L)

1 large Chinese or napa cabbage

Coarse salt

MARINADE

1 large carrot, peeled and julienned

1 small red apple (such as Gala), cored and julienned

5 scallions, 3 small leeks (white and green parts), or 1 small bunch fresh chives, chopped

5 garlic cloves, minced

1 medium white onion, chopped

One ¾-inch (2 cm) piece fresh ginger, chopped

3 tablespoons sweet rice flour

About ¾ cup (150 g) gochugaru (ground or flakes)

(Tips:) **Depending on the room temperature, kimchi needs between 12 hours and 3 days to ferment. The flavors will continue to develop once it is stored in the fridge. The kimchi should always be kept in an airtight container, both during the fermenting process and once in the fridge to avoid spoilage.**

Once it has fermented, you can start eating kimchi at any time, although it takes about 2 weeks in the refrigerator to fully develop its flavors. Kimchi will continue to age in the refrigerator and will remain delicious for several months. It will get more sour over time, but it can still be used in numerous dishes.

Korean Cucumber Kimchi

Cucumber kimchi (oi kimchi, 오이 김치) is very popular in Korea, and happens to be my favorite kind of kimchi. In three words, it's crunchy, light, and tasty.

1. Sprinkle the cucumber slices with coarse salt. Place on a paper or kitchen towel and allow to sit for 20 minutes, until they have released their liquid. Transfer to a sieve and rinse under cold water to remove excess salt. Drain well and place in a medium bowl.

2. Add the carrot, onion, and scallions to the cucumber.

3. To make the marinade, combine the garlic, ginger, gochugaru, vinegar, sugar, and sesame oil to taste in a small bowl. Stir well.

4. Add the marinade to the vegetables and stir. Transfer the kimchi to a glass bowl or 32-ounce/1-quart (1 L) glass preserving jar, pressing down lightly to release air pockets. Cover and keep at room temperature for approximately 30 hours. Once fermented, keep refrigerated, covered.

1 large English cucumber, thinly sliced

Coarse salt

1 medium carrot, peeled and julienned

1 medium white onion, thinly sliced

1 scallion, 1 small leek (white and green parts), or 1 small bunch fresh chives, finely chopped

MARINADE

2 garlic cloves, minced

One 2½- to 3-inch (6–8 cm) piece fresh ginger, chopped

¼ cup (50 g) gochugaru (ground or flakes)

2 tablespoons rice vinegar

1 tablespoon superfine sugar

1 to 2 tablespoons toasted sesame oil

(Tips:) Depending on the room temperature, kimchi needs between 12 hours and 3 days to ferment. The flavors will continue to develop once it is stored in the fridge. The kimchi should always be kept in an airtight container, both during the fermenting process and once in the fridge to avoid spoilage.

Once it has fermented, you can start eating kimchi at any time, although it takes about 2 weeks in the refrigerator to fully develop its flavors. Kimchi will continue to age in the refrigerator and will remain delicious for several months. It will get more sour over time, but it can still be used in numerous dishes.

KOREAN
CUCUMBER
KIMCHI
(PAGE 15)

CHINESE
CABBAGE
KIMCHI
(PAGE 14)

"Oyster" Sauce

Oyster sauce is a thick brown sauce commonly used in southern China, made from leftover oyster cooking liquid. The sauce was invented by accident in 1888, when Lee Kum Sheung, the owner of a Chinese food kiosk, let a pot of oyster soup boil for so long that it turned into a thick brown paste. He named it "oyster sauce" and began serving it to his customers as a condiment, later bottling and selling it under the now widespread brand name Lee Kum Kee.

As for flavor, it's a mixture of sweet and salty, but the overall flavor is umami. In China, the word to describe umami is xiān wèi (鲜味). Personally, I can't do without this ingredient—especially in stir-fries. Here is my recipe for a vegan oyster sauce.

1. Place the mushrooms in a large bowl and add the hot water. Make sure the mushrooms are completely submerged. Allow to soak for 1 hour.

2. Pour the mushrooms with their soaking water into a blender and blend until liquefied.

3. Pour the mushroom purée into a small saucepan. Add the soy sauce, agave syrup, miso, and ginger, and whisk over medium heat until it starts to boil. Turn down the heat and simmer to reduce, about 10 minutes.

4. Pour the cornstarch slurry into the saucepan, stirring briskly. Simmer for 5 minutes until the sauce thickens.

5. Allow to cool and store in a tightly capped bottle or glass preserving jar.

MAKES ABOUT 3 CUPS (720 ML)

5.25 ounces (150 g) dried shiitake mushrooms, stems removed

1¾ cups (420 ml) plus 2 tablespoons hot water

3 tablespoons light soy sauce

3 tablespoons agave syrup

1 tablespoon white miso

1 teaspoon grated fresh ginger

2 teaspoons cornstarch mixed with 2 tablespoons cold water to make a slurry

Tip: This will keep for several weeks in the refrigerator, tightly capped.

"Fish" Sauce

Few ingredients add as much flavor to a dish as fish sauce. It's sweet and salty, with a real wave of umami flavors. This seafood-based sauce of fermented fish is used very often in Southeast Asian cuisine, especially in Vietnam and Thailand, in dishes such as green papaya salad and bò bún, but also in stir-fries, in pad thai, and more.

With this sauce as a base, you can make a very popular condiment called nuoc mam, made from fish sauce, garlic, red chile, sugar, and vinegar. This sauce is often served with Vietnamese summer rolls. I've developed a "fish" sauce that is 100 percent vegetable based.

1. In a large saucepan, combine 2 tablespoons of the brown sugar and the pineapple chunks. Cook over low heat for about 10 minutes, stirring occasionally, until the sugar has melted and the pineapple caramelizes.

2. Add 1 quart (1 L) water, the wakame, mushrooms, soy sauce, salt, and the remaining brown sugar to the pineapple and bring to a boil.

3. Turn down the heat and simmer for 30 minutes, until the mixture thickens and the pineapple begins to caramelize again. Adjust sugar and salt to taste.

4. Strain the "fish" sauce into a jar, let cool, and cover. (Reserve the pineapple and mushrooms for another use, if desired.)

MAKES 1.5 QUARTS (1.5 L)

- ¼ cup (50 g) brown sugar, plus more if needed
- 1 ripe pineapple, peeled, cored, and chopped
- 2 tablespoons (10 g) wakame, rehydrated and drained
- 5 dried shiitake mushrooms, stems removed
- ¼ cup (60 ml) plus 1 tablespoon light soy sauce
- 2 tablespoons salt, plus more if needed

(Tip:) **This keeps in the refrigerator, tightly capped, for up to 2 weeks.**

Homemade Udon Noodles

These udon noodles are made from a few ingredients: all-purpose flour, water, salt, and cornstarch. Udon noodles are very popular in Japan as they are so versatile, and you can serve them in various ways, such as in soup, with sauce, sautéed, in salad, or in a hot or cold dish. The most well-known dishes containing udon noodles are: tempura udon (udon noodles in a simple broth with tempura), nikutama udon (udon noodles in a sweet broth with meat), and Yaki Udon (fried udon noodles; page 71).

MAKES 4 SERVINGS

¾ cup (180 ml) plus
  2 tablespoons ice water

1 tablespoon fine salt

3⅓ cups (400 g) all-purpose flour

¼ cup (30 g) cornstarch

(Tip:) What's great about this recipe is that you can make several portions in advance and freeze the uncooked noodles for future use.

1. In a small bowl, combine the water and salt. Stir until completely dissolved.

2. Place the flour in a large bowl. Set aside 2 tablespoons of the salt water and add the remaining ¾ cup (180 ml) to the flour. Mix with your fingertips to combine into a shaggy dough.

3. Add the reserved 2 tablespoons salt water and knead with the palms of your hands and thumbs, slowly forming the mixture into a ball of dough.

4. Place the dough in a heavy-duty plastic bag and flatten by pressing down on the bag with a rolling pin. Roll it out to a disk about 8 inches (20 cm) in diameter. Remove the dough from the bag, fold into a semicircle, then roll it back into a ball. Repeat this operation 20 times. Put it back in the bag and allow to rest in a warm place for 30 minutes.

5. Remove the dough from the bag and place it on a work surface dusted with the cornstarch. Roll the ball flat with a rolling pin until it's ¼-inch (6 mm) thick. Fold the dough in half and cut into ⅛-inch-wide (3 mm) strips.

6. Gather the noodles in your hands and shake them lightly to remove any excess cornstarch. Gently separate the noodles.

7. To cook, bring a pot of water to a boil. Add the noodles and cook for about 5 minutes, until tender.

Cold Noodle Soups

Cold Noodles * NAENGMYEON

In Korea, cold noodles are very popular, and naengmyeon is the most popular noodle dish of all. Literally translated, the name means "cold noodles." You make this dish with thin buckwheat and sweet potato noodles, a refreshing broth, and various condiments. There are two kinds of naengmyeon: mul naengmyeon and bibim naengmyeon—the most noticeable difference is that this bibim version is sprinkled with a generous amount of very hot red sauce.

1. To make the sauce, combine ¼ cup (60 ml) water with the gochugaru, pear, sugar, garlic, soy sauce, and salt in a small bowl. Mix well, then chill until you're ready to serve.

2. Bring a pot of water to a boil and cook the noodles according to the package instructions until tender, 3 to 5 minutes. Drain, then rinse the noodles under cold water to prevent them from cooking further, until they are cold to the touch. Drain well. Divide equally between two deep bowls.

3. In a small bowl, combine the vegetable stock, vinegar, and sugar. Mix well, then ladle half into each bowl of noodles. Add 3 or 4 ice cubes to each bowl. Garnish each with the cucumber, radish, a slice or two of pear (I recommend two), the sliced scallion, sesame seeds, and sesame oil. Serve the sauce on the side, for dipping, or pour 4 to 6 tablespoons of the sauce (according to your taste) over each serving.

SERVES 2

HOT NAENGMYEON BIMBIM SAUCE

¼ cup (65 g) gochugaru (ground or flakes)

3 tablespoons grated peeled pear or Korean apple

2 tablespoons superfine sugar

2 teaspoons minced garlic

1 tablespoon light soy sauce

1 teaspoon fine salt

NOODLES

8 ounces (227 g) naengmyeon (buckwheat and potato) noodles

2 cups (480 ml) cold Vegetable Dashi (page 12) or vegetable broth

1 tablespoon plus 1 teaspoon rice vinegar

1 teaspoon superfine sugar

6 to 8 ice cubes

GARNISH

½ small English cucumber, peeled if desired, cut into matchsticks

1 small daikon radish, peeled and thinly sliced

2 to 4 thin slices peeled pear or Asian pear

1 scallion (green parts only), thinly sliced

1 teaspoon sesame seeds

2 tablespoons toasted sesame oil

Cold Noodle Soup with Soy Milk * KONGGUKSU

Very popular in Korea in the summertime, this refreshing
noodle dish only has five ingredients: cucumber, yellow
soybeans, noodles, salt, and water. This dish's main ingredient
is homemade soy milk, served chilled over thin noodles.
You need to soak the soybeans, so you'll want to plan ahead.
Once the beans are soaked, they are simply cooked and
blended, then everything comes together in 30 minutes! Serve
with Chinese Cabbage Kimchi (page 14), Korean Cucumber
Kimchi (page 15), or another favorite side dish.

1. Cook the soybeans for 20 minutes in 2 cups (480 ml) water,
   until soft.

2. Drain the soybeans and add to a blender with the pine nuts,
   2 tablespoons of the sesame seeds, the salt, and another
   2 cups (480 ml) water. Blend until smooth and creamy.
   Refrigerate for 30 minutes.

3. Bring a pot of water to a boil and cook the noodles according
   to the package instructions until tender, 3 to 4 minutes.
   Drain, then rinse the noodles under cold water to prevent
   them from cooking further, until they are cold to the touch.
   Drain well. Divide equally between two deep bowls.

4. Pour the soy milk over the noodles. Garnish with the
   cucumber, tomato, the remaining sesame seeds, and 3 or
   4 ice cubes.

SERVES 2

¼ cup (90 g) yellow soybeans,
soaked overnight in cold water
and drained

2 tablespoons pine nuts

2 tablespoons sesame seeds, plus
2 tablespoons for serving

1 teaspoon fine salt

8 ounces (227 g) thin noodles
(such as somen noodles)

1 small English cucumber, peeled
and cut into matchsticks, for
serving

½ small plum tomato, seeded and
cut into matchsticks, for serving

6 to 8 ice cubes

Cold Noodle Soup with Kimchi * KIMCHIMARI GUKSU

Cold noodle soup with kimchi, or kimchimari guksu, is a deliciously irresistible, refreshing, spicy, and tangy soup—just the way I like it. The essential ingredient, of course, is kimchi! Its juice holds all the flavor necessary to make this dish nice and spicy.

1. To prepare the soup, combine ¼ cup (60 ml) water with the vegetable dashi, kimchi juice, vinegar, sugar, and soy sauce in a large bowl. Refrigerate until completely chilled, about 1 hour.

2. Bring a pot of water to a boil and cook the noodles according to the package instructions until tender, about 4 minutes. Drain, then rinse the noodles under cold water to prevent them from cooking further, until they are cold to the touch. Drain well. Divide equally between two deep bowls.

3. Chop the kimchi into 2-inch (5 cm) chunks. Place in a medium bowl, add the sesame oil, sugar, garlic, and sesame seeds, and mix together.

4. To assemble, pour the soup over the noodles, add the kimchi seasoning, cucumber, nori, and ice cubes, and sprinkle with the sesame seeds. Serve cold.

SERVES 2

SOUP

1 cup (240 ml) Vegetable Dashi (page 12) or vegetable broth

¼ cup (60 ml) juice from Chinese Cabbage Kimchi (page 14)

1 tablespoon rice vinegar

1 tablespoon superfine sugar

1 tablespoon light soy sauce

3½ ounces (100 g) somen noodles

KIMCHI SEASONING

¾ cup (110 g) Chinese Cabbage Kimchi (page 14)

1 tablespoon toasted sesame oil

1 teaspoon superfine sugar

2 garlic cloves, chopped

1 tablespoon sesame seeds

GARNISH

½ English cucumber, peeled if desired, cut into matchsticks

1 tablespoon nori seaweed flakes or small strips

6 to 8 ice cubes

1 tablespoon sesame seeds

Sudachi Soba

Sudachi is a Japanese citrus fruit that is harvested when still green to preserve its acidity. In Japan, the fruit is often paired with soba noodles to create a delicious dish full of umami. The ingredients are very simple, which is why a good dashi broth is of the utmost importance. Check your local specialty or Asian grocery store for sudachi—if you can't find them, limes will work just as well in this recipe.

1. In a medium bowl, dissolve the dashi and salt in the hot water. Add the soy sauce and ice water and stir to combine. Cover and refrigerate until you're ready to serve.

2. Bring a pot of water to a boil and cook the noodles according to the package instructions until tender, about 5 minutes. Drain, then rinse the noodles under cold water to prevent them from cooking further, until they are cold to the touch. Drain well. Divide equally between two deep bowls.

3. Pour the cold broth over the noodles. Garnish each bowl with half of the radish, the ice cubes, and sudachi slices, and serve.

SERVES 2

BROTH

3 tablespoons granulated vegan dashi

1 tablespoon salt

5 tablespoons hot water

2 tablespoons light soy sauce

1⅔ cups (400 ml) ice water

8 ounces (227 g) soba (buckwheat) noodles

GARNISH

2 tablespoons grated daikon radish

6 to 8 ice cubes

1 sudachi or lime, thinly sliced

(Tip:) **To save time, you can make the broth the night before—it's just as fresh the day after preparation.**

Cold Somen

When it's very hot outside, I usually crave a good bowl of cold somen soaked in a delicious tsuyu sauce. Trust me, you'll love it.

1. To make the tsuyu sauce, combine the sake, mirin, soy sauce, kombu, and shiitake mushrooms in a saucepan and bring to a boil. Simmer for 5 minutes, then strain into a medium bowl. (Reserve the kombu and shiitake for another use, if desired.) Allow to cool to room temperature. Dilute the sauce with the ice water. Refrigerate until you're ready to serve.

2. Bring a pot of water to a boil and cook the noodles according to the package instructions until tender, about 4 minutes. Drain, then rinse the noodles under cold water to prevent them from cooking further, until they are cold to the touch. Drain well. Divide equally between two deep bowls.

3. Place 3 or 4 ice cubes in each bowl of noodles. Pour the sauce over the noodles and top with the ginger and sliced scallion. Serve cold.

SERVES 2

TSUYU SAUCE

½ cup (120 ml) sake

1 cup (240 ml) plus 2 tablespoons mirin

1 cup (240 ml) light soy sauce

1 sheet kombu

2 dried shiitake mushrooms, stems removed, rehydrated

1 cup (240 ml) ice water

8 ounces (227 g) somen noodles

6 to 8 ice cubes

GARNISH

One ¼-inch (6 mm) piece fresh ginger, finely julienned

1 scallion (white and green parts), thinly sliced

Tip: If you have Soup Stock (Mentsuyu) (page 13) in your fridge, you can dilute 2½ cups (600 ml) of it with 1 cup (240 ml) ice water, plus a few ice cubes. Use this instead of the tsuyu sauce, so you can make and enjoy this dish even faster!

Cold Noodle Salads

Zaru Soba

The best ways to eat soba noodles, in my opinion, are in the dishes zaru soba or mori soba, a variation that omits the nori. It's a very popular summer dish in Japan. Zaru soba are traditionally served on a bamboo mat called a "zaru." They are accompanied by various condiments, as well as a sauce for dipping the noodles.

1. To make the sauce, combine the vegetable dashi, soy sauce, mirin, and sugar in a small saucepan and bring to a boil. Boil for 1 to 2 minutes. Remove from the heat and pour into a small bowl. Add the chopped scallion. Place in the refrigerator to cool.

2. Bring a large pot of water to a boil and cook the noodles according to the package instructions until tender, about 5 minutes. Drain, then rinse the noodles under cold water to prevent them from cooking further, until they are cold to the touch. Drain well. Divide equally between two large plates or bamboo mats and sprinkle with the nori.

3. Divide the sauce between two small bowls and add 3 or 4 ice cubes to keep it cold. Divide the sliced scallion and the wasabi between two small plates. Serve the sauce and garnish plates alongside the noodles.

SERVES 2

DIPPING SAUCE

1 cup (240 ml) Vegetable Dashi (page 12) or vegetable broth

¼ cup (60 ml) light soy sauce

¼ cup (60 ml) mirin

1 teaspoon superfine sugar

1 scallion (white and green parts), finely chopped

8 ounces (227 g) soba (buckwheat) noodles

2 tablespoons shredded nori seaweed

6 to 8 ice cubes

GARNISH

1 scallion (green part only), thinly sliced

2 dabs wasabi paste

Cold Ramen * HIYASHI CHUKA

There are many noodle recipes that appeal to me in the summer, and one of them is hiyashi chuka. It's a cold noodle dish of Japanese origin, topped with an assortment of raw vegetables (you can use whatever you have on hand or simply the ones you like the most), and a delicious sauce with either a sesame or soy sauce base. This is not traditionally a vegan dish—it is usually topped with meat, which I replace here with firm tofu.

1. To make the dressing, combine the sesame seeds, vegetable dashi, soy sauce, tahini, mirin, rice vinegar, and sesame oil in a small bowl or pitcher. Mix well. Refrigerate for at least 30 minutes, until you're ready to serve.

2. Bring a pot of water to a boil and cook the noodles according to the package instructions until tender, about 2 minutes. Drain, then rinse the noodles under cold water to prevent them from cooking further, until they are cold to the touch. Drain well. Divide equally between two plates or shallow soup bowls, placing the noodles in the center.

3. To serve, arrange the tomato, bell pepper, cucumber, carrot, tofu, and corn on top of the noodles. Pour over the dressing and sprinkle with sesame seeds.

SERVES 2

DRESSING

2 teaspoons sesame seeds

¼ cup (60 ml) Vegetable Dashi (page 12) or vegetable broth

1 tablespoon light soy sauce

2 teaspoons sesame paste (tahini)

1 teaspoon mirin

1 teaspoon rice vinegar

1 teaspoon toasted sesame oil

8 ounces (227 g) rice noodles or ramen noodles

GARNISH

½ small plum tomato, seeded and cut into matchsticks

½ red bell pepper, seeded and cut into matchsticks

½ English cucumber, peeled and cut into matchsticks

1 small carrot, cut into matchsticks

Half an 8-ounce (226 g) block smoked firm tofu, cut into matchsticks

¼ cup (45 g) plus 1 tablespoon cooked corn kernels

Sesame seeds

COLD NOODLE SALADS

Soba Salad with Spicy Peanut Dressing

Soba noodles are made from buckwheat, which has an earthy and slightly nutty flavor. Peanut pairs perfectly with them. This noodle salad is refreshing, tasty, and gluten-free, plus it's nutritious, too.

1. Bring a pot of water to a boil and cook the noodles according to the package instructions until tender, about 5 minutes. Drain, then rinse the noodles under cold water to prevent them from cooking further, until they are cold to the touch. Set aside to drain well.

2. To prepare the dressing, combine 3 tablespoons water with the peanut butter, soy sauce, garlic, vinegar, maple syrup, crushed peanuts, and sriracha in a small bowl. Mix well.

3. In a large bowl, place the noodles, cucumber, red cabbage, carrot, and scallions. Pour over the dressing and toss until well coated. Garnish with the cilantro and crushed peanuts. Chill in the refrigerator until you're ready to serve.

SERVES 4

14 ounces (397 g) soba (buckwheat) noodles

DRESSING

¼ cup (60 g) peanut butter

2 tablespoons light soy sauce

2 garlic cloves, minced

1 tablespoon rice vinegar

1 tablespoon maple syrup

1 tablespoon crushed peanuts

1 tablespoon sriracha

½ English cucumber, cut into matchsticks

¾ cup (50 g) shredded red cabbage

1 small carrot, peeled and cut into matchsticks

2 scallions, 1 small leek (white and green parts), or 1 small bunch fresh chives, coarsely chopped

Fresh cilantro sprigs, for serving

3 tablespoons crushed peanuts, for serving

Vietnamese Noodle Salad · BÚN BÒ XÀO

This Vietnamese noodle salad abounds in fresh herbs, delicious condiments, and a refreshing dressing. Topped with crunchy deep-fried Vietnamese spring rolls, it's the perfect combination of flavors and textures! It only takes half an hour to prepare, and you can enjoy it as a main course or a side.

1. To make the vegan nuoc mam, in a small bowl, combine 2 tablespoons water with the white vinegar, chile, sugar, soy sauce, and garlic. Mix well. Refrigerate until you're ready to serve.

2. To cook the tofu, in a frying pan, heat the oil over medium heat. Add the tofu, bell pepper, and onion and sauté for 2 to 3 minutes until the vegetables soften slightly. Add the garlic, soy sauce, and lemongrass. Continue to cook for 2 to 3 minutes, until the tofu is nicely browned. Remove from the heat and allow to cool.

3. To cook the spring rolls, fill a deep pot halfway with vegetable oil. Deep-fry the spring rolls according to the package instructions. Set aside to drain on paper towels. Cut each spring roll in half on the diagonal.

4. Bring a pot of water to a boil and cook the noodles according to the package instructions until tender, 2 to 3 minutes. Drain, then rinse the noodles under cold water to prevent them from cooking further, until they are cold to the touch. Drain well.

5. To serve, line the bottom of two deep soup bowls with lettuce leaves, then add the rice vermicelli in the middle. Place half the carrots, the cucumber, spring roll pieces, mint leaves, and tomato (if using) around the edges of each bowl. Top with the tofu mixture and sprinkle with the peanuts and sliced scallion. Divide the nuoc mam between two small bowls and serve on the side.

SERVES 2

VEGAN NUOC MAM

2 tablespoons white vinegar

1 tablespoon minced red chile pepper

1 tablespoon superfine sugar

2 tablespoons light soy sauce

2 garlic cloves, minced

TOFU

4 teaspoons vegetable oil or other neutral oil

One 12-ounce (340 g) block firm tofu, pressed and cut into matchsticks

1 small red bell pepper, seeded and cut into thin matchsticks

1 small onion, thinly sliced

2 garlic cloves, coarsely chopped

2 tablespoons light soy sauce

1 teaspoon minced lemongrass (white part only)

Vegetable or other neutral oil, for deep-frying

6 store-bought vegan spring rolls

8 ounces (227 g) rice vermicelli noodles

GARNISH

A few green leaf or butter lettuce leaves

1 small carrot, peeled and cut into matchsticks

½ English cucumber, halved lengthwise and cut diagonally in thin slices

Leaves from 2 mint sprigs

1 small plum tomato, seeded and finely chopped (optional)

2 tablespoons chopped peanuts

1 scallion or 1 small leek (white and light green parts), finely chopped

Summer Rolls * GỎI CUỐN

Gỏi cuốn literally translates to "salad rolls," though for a long time I didn't make the connection between these and summer rolls. These are made up of a mixture of salad, herbs, various raw vegetables, tofu (or any protein of your choice), and rice noodles. Dip them in as much sauce as you like and have a feast! There are dozens of different sauces you can pair with these summer rolls, but personally I prefer a peanut butter–hoisin sauce; I promise once you taste it, you'll realize how irresistible it is. I love summer rolls. They are fun to eat and perfect for a dinner with friends—let everyone choose their favorite ingredients and roll up right at the table!

1. Heat the sesame oil in a frying pan over medium heat. Add the tofu and sauté, 1 to 2 minutes. Add the soy sauce and sugar. Once the tofu has turned golden brown, remove from the heat and set aside to cool.

2. Bring a pot of water to a boil and cook the noodles according to the package instructions until tender, 2 to 3 minutes. Drain, then rinse the noodles under cold water to prevent them from cooking further, until they are cold to the touch. Set aside to drain well.

3. Pour warm water onto a plate. Working with one sheet of rice paper at a time, dip the paper in the water for about 5 seconds—no more, or it will tear. Lay the soaked rice paper on the work surface. Place 1 lettuce leaf on the rice paper, then place a small portion each of the mint, cilantro, tofu, carrot, avocado, cucumber, cabbage, and rice vermicelli on the center of the lettuce leaf. Fold the bottom edge of the rice paper up and over the filling, fold in the sides, and continue to roll it like a burrito. Set aside on a large plate and cover loosely. Repeat with the remaining sheets of rice paper and filling, to create 10 rolls.

4. Serve with hoisin sauce, lettuce, and the extra mint and cilantro leaves.

SERVES 2

TOFU

2 teaspoons toasted sesame oil

Half a 14-ounce (397 g) block firm tofu, pressed and cut into matchsticks

2 teaspoons light soy sauce

1 teaspoon superfine sugar

ROLLS

8 ounces (227 g) rice vermicelli noodles

10 sheets rice paper

10 butter lettuce or green leaf lettuce leaves, plus more for serving

Leaves from 5 mint sprigs, shredded, plus more for serving

Leaves from 5 cilantro sprigs, plus more for serving

1 small carrot, cut into thin matchsticks

1 avocado, pitted, peeled, and thinly sliced

½ English cucumber, cut into thin matchsticks

1½ cups (100 g) shredded red cabbage

½ cup (150 g) hoisin sauce, store-bought or homemade (recipe follows)

(Tip:) If you're preparing the rolls ahead of time, place them on a plate covered with parchment paper, so they don't stick, and cover them with a damp cloth. Store in the refrigerator.

Homemade Hoisin Sauce

2 tablespoons toasted sesame oil

4 garlic cloves, crushed into
a paste

⅓ cup (80 g) plus 1 tablespoon
peanut butter

¼ cup (60 ml) light soy sauce

2 tablespoons rice vinegar

1 teaspoon red chile paste
(such as harissa or gochujang)

3 grinds of black pepper

Heat the sesame oil in a small saucepan over medium heat. Add the garlic and cook until browned, 3 to 4 minutes. Add 3 tablespoons water, the peanut butter, soy sauce, vinegar, chile paste, and black pepper. Stir to combine. Once the mixture starts to boil, turn off the heat. Allow to cool to room temperature, then transfer to a small glass preserving jar, cover, and refrigerate.

Cellophane Noodle Salad * YUM WOON SEN

Yum woon sen is a dish as popular abroad as it is in Thailand. I love the way the nearly transparent noodles soak up the spicy sauce, and how the peanuts add a pleasant crunch. Many people in Thailand consider mung bean noodles (also called cellophane noodles) as a health food and a healthy alternative to other types of noodles. And since you don't need many noodles to fill a bowl, the dish is low in calories!

1. In a small frying pan, toast the peanuts in a drizzle of oil for 4 to 5 minutes. Remove from the heat and transfer to a small plate to cool to room temperature. Place the peanuts in a resealable plastic bag and use a rolling pin to crush them.

2. Bring a small pot of water to a boil. Place the noodles in a medium bowl and pour over with the boiling water. Soak for 6 minutes, stirring occasionally to prevent the noodles from sticking together. Drain well and return to the bowl. Cut the noodles a few times with kitchen shears, so they are more manageable.

3. To make the dressing, in a small bowl, combine the vinegar, lime juice, superfine sugar, garlic powder, and onion. Add chile to taste. Mix well.

4. Transfer the noodles to a serving bowl. Add the bell peppers, tomato, and cilantro. Pour over the dressing and mix gently. Sprinkle with the peanuts and serve.

SERVES 2

⅓ cup (100 g) raw peanuts

Vegetable oil or other neutral oil, for toasting

8 ounces (227 g) mung bean (cellophane) noodles

DRESSING

2 tablespoons rice vinegar

Juice of 1 lime (2 to 3 tablespoons)

1 tablespoon superfine sugar

1 tablespoon garlic powder

½ small onion, minced

1 red Thai chile pepper (bird's eye chile), minced

GARNISH

½ small green bell pepper, seeded and cut into matchsticks

½ small red bell pepper, seeded and cut into matchsticks

1 or 2 small plum tomato, quartered and seeded, each quarter cut into thin slices

Leaves from 5 or 6 fresh cilantro sprigs

(Tip:) This salad should be eaten as soon as it's made, because the noodles are very absorbent and will become pasty if they sit in the dressing for too long.

Cold Peanut Butter Noodles

Peanut butter noodles are going to become your go-to recipe once you realize how easy they are to prepare and how irresistible their flavor is. All you need to make this scrumptious peanut dressing are a few basic staples that you probably already have in your pantry. This dressing pairs well with any Asian noodle, so choose your favorite and enjoy!

1. To make the dressing, heat the oil in a frying pan over medium heat. Add the garlic and scallions and cook until they begin to brown. Add ¼ cup (60 ml) water, the sugar, gochugaru, soy sauce, and peanut butter. Stir to create a smooth and creamy consistency. Remove from the heat, pour into a large bowl, and set aside to cool.

2. Bring a pot of water to a boil and cook the noodles according to the package instructions until tender, 2 to 5 minutes. (Or follow the directions on page 20 if you are using homemade udon noodles.) Drain, then rinse under cold water to prevent the noodles from cooking further, until they are cold to the touch. Drain well.

3. Add the noodles to the dressing and mix well. If the dressing is too thick, add a little more water.

4. Garnish with the sliced scallion and crushed peanuts and serve.

SERVES 1

DRESSING

- 3 tablespoons vegetable oil or other neutral oil
- 3 garlic cloves, minced
- 2 scallions or 1 small leek (white and green parts), finely chopped
- 1 tablespoon superfine sugar
- 1 tablespoon gochugaru (ground or flakes)
- 2 tablespoons light soy sauce
- 3 tablespoons peanut butter

- 3.5 ounces (100 g) wheat noodles (such as ramen)

GARNISH

- 1 scallion or small leek (green parts only), thinly sliced
- 1 tablespoon crushed peanuts

(Tip:) You can also serve these noodles warm; cook and drain the noodles as soon as the dressing is done and mix them together while both are warm.

Summer Rolls With Spicy Noodles

This is a combination of my two favorite recipes: summer rolls and spicy noodles. One day I decided to use up some spicy noodles by rolling them into a piece of rice paper along with some vegetables, and ever since it's been one of my obsessions!

1. In a medium heat-safe bowl, combine the gochugaru, gochujang, sesame seeds, salt, garlic, and scallions. Heat the oil in a small saucepan over medium heat, then slowly pour into the gochugaru mixture. (The oil will sizzle—that's normal!) Mix well. Set aside a few tablespoons of the sauce in a small bowl for serving.

2. Bring a pot of water to a boil and cook the noodles according to the package instructions until tender, about 4 minutes. Drain, then rinse the noodles under cold water to prevent them from cooking further, until they are cold to the touch. Drain well.

3. Add the noodles to the medium bowl of sauce and toss until the noodles are well coated.

4. Pour warm water onto a plate. Working with one sheet of rice paper at a time, dip the paper in the water for about 5 seconds—no more, or it will tear. Lay the soaked rice paper on the work surface. Place 1 lettuce leaf on the rice paper, then add a small portion of the avocado, carrot, and spicy noodles. Fold the bottom edge of the rice paper up and over the filling, fold in the sides, and continue to roll it like a burrito. Set aside on a large plate and cover loosely. Repeat with the remaining sheets of rice paper and filling, to create 10 rolls.

5. Line plates with lettuce leaves and top with the rolls. Sprinkle with the chopped scallion and sesame seeds (if using) and serve right away!

SERVES 2

SPICY SAUCE

- 3 tablespoons gochugaru (ground or flakes)
- 1 tablespoon gochujang
- 1 teaspoon sesame seeds, plus more for serving (optional)
- 1 teaspoon coarse salt
- 4 garlic cloves, minced
- 3 scallions, 1 small leek (white and green parts), or 1 small bunch fresh chives, finely chopped, plus more for serving
- 3 tablespoons vegetable oil or other neutral oil

ROLLS

- 8 ounces (227 g) somen noodles
- 10 pieces rice paper
- 10 butter lettuce or green leaf lettuce leaves, plus more for serving
- 1 avocado, peeled, pitted and thinly sliced
- 1 small carrot, peeled and cut into matchsticks

(Tip:) If you're preparing the rolls ahead of time, place them on parchment paper, so they don't stick, and cover them with a damp cloth. Garnish when you serve them.

COLD NOODLE SALADS

Spicy Cold Skin Noodles * LIANGPI

Liangpi is a very popular noodle dish in northwestern China, usually served cold. Liangpi has a slippery and unique stretchy texture.

1. Cook the noodles according to package instructions. Drain, rinse well under cold water, and drain again.

2. To make the spicy oil, mix the gochugaru, salt, sesame seeds, and garlic in a medium heat-safe bowl. Heat the oil, bay leaves, Sichuan peppercorns, star anise, cinnamon, and ginger in a small saucepan over medium heat for about 5 minutes. Remove from the heat and carefully strain the hot oil into the gochugaru mixture bit by bit, so it doesn't splash. (Discard the spices.) Allow to rest for 2 to 3 minutes, then add the vinegar and mix well.

3. Add a few tablespoons of the spicy oil to the noodles, to taste, and gently toss to coat well. Top with the cucumber and bean sprouts. Sprinkle with a few cilantro leaves, if using, and serve.

SERVES 2

8 ounces (227 g) store-bought liangpi noodles or dried wide rice noodles or mung bean (cellophane) noodles

SPICY OIL

¼ cup (50 g) gochugaru (ground or flakes)

1 tablespoon salt

⅓ cup (40 g) sesame seeds

6 garlic cloves, minced

1¼ cup (300 ml) vegetable oil or other neutral oil

2 bay leaves

10 Sichuan peppercorns

2 star anise

1 small cinnamon stick

2 thin slices fresh ginger

2 tablespoons black vinegar

GARNISH

½ English cucumber, halved lengthwise and thinly sliced

1 small handful of bean sprouts

Fresh cilantro leaves (optional)

(Tip:) Transfer any unused spicy oil to a bottle or glass preserving jar, cap tightly, and store in the refrigerator for up to 1 month.

Kimchi Spicy Noodles * KIMCHI BIBIM GUKSU

What to cook when there's nothing in the refrigerator? In Korea, kimchi is a kitchen staple, making it the go-to ingredient when this question arises. So if you have a jar of kimchi on hand (I always keep one), try this kimchi bibim guksu (김치비빔국수) for a quick lunch or light meal. It's spicy, sweet, tart, and crunchy thanks to the kimchi—as you'll soon find out, it's delicious. Kimchi is really all you need to make this dish, to which you can add various condiments. You can also add other vegetables such as cucumber, Korean Cucumber Kimchi (page 15), or lettuce.

1. Bring a pot of water to a boil and cook the noodles according to the package instructions until tender, 3 to 4 minutes. Drain, then rinse the noodles under cold water to prevent them from cooking further, until they are cold to the touch. Set aside to drain well.

2. To make the dressing, in a medium bowl, combine the kimchi, kimchi juice, gochujang, soy sauce, vinegar, sugar, sesame oil, and sesame seeds. Mix well.

3. Add the noodles to the kimchi dressing and gently toss until the noodles are well coated. Adjust seasoning to taste, adding more soy sauce, sugar, and/or vinegar, if necessary. Top with cucumber, cucumber kimchi, sliced scallions, sesame seeds, and lettuce. Serve cold.

SERVES 2

8 ounces (227 g) somyeon (thin wheat) noodles or somen noodles

DRESSING

1¾ cups (250 g) thinly sliced Chinese Cabbage Kimchi (page 14), plus ¼ cup (60 ml) juice

1 tablespoon gochujang

1 tablespoon light soy sauce

2 tablespoons rice vinegar

2 tablespoons superfine sugar

1 tablespoon toasted sesame oil

2 teaspoons sesame seeds, plus more for serving (optional)

GARNISH (OPTIONAL)

⅓ English cucumber, cut into matchsticks

½ cup (105 g) Korean Cucumber Kimchi (page 15)

2 scallions (green part only), thinly sliced

A few butter lettuce or green leaf lettuce leaves

Rolled Rice Noodles * CHEUNG FUN

Cheung fun is a roll made with rice noodles. It's a Cantonese dish served as a snack or as dim sum. The dish is served for breakfast or brunch, accompanied by a delicious soy-based sauce that is as sweet as it is salty. Here, I'm going to show you how you can make these noodles in no time. The key to this recipe is to use a microwave-safe baking dish.

1. To make the noodles, combine ⅓ cup (80 ml) water with the rice flour, tapioca flour, cornstarch, sesame oil, and salt in a medium bowl. Stir until a thick batter forms, adding more water if necessary.

2. Using a pastry brush, lightly coat a large glass microwave-safe baking dish with vegetable oil. Cover with a thin layer of the noodle batter. Cook in the microwave on high for approximately 1 minute, until the noodle is set. Allow to cool until safe to handle, about 1 minute. Remove the noodle sheet from the baking dish and set aside on a large plate. Repeat with the remaining noodle batter, placing a sheet of parchment paper between each layer.

3. To make the sauce, heat 1 teaspoon of the sesame oil in a frying pan over medium heat. Add the garlic and sliced scallion. Once they start to brown, add ¼ cup (60 ml) water, the soy sauce, sugar, and the remaining sesame oil. When the sugar has melted, the sauce is ready.

4. Roll the noodles and divide equally between two plates. Drizzle the sauce over top. Garnish with the sliced scallion, if using, and serve.

SERVES 2

NOODLES

¾ cup (125 g) sweet rice flour

½ cup (60 g) tapioca flour

1 teaspoon cornstarch

1 teaspoon toasted sesame oil

1 teaspoon salt

Vegetable oil or other neutral oil, for greasing the baking dish

SAUCE

3 tablespoons toasted sesame oil, plus more for frying

3 garlic cloves, minced

1 scallion or small leek (white and green parts), finely chopped, plus more, sliced, for serving (optional)

2 tablespoons light soy sauce

2 teaspoons superfine sugar

Sautéed
Noodles

Noodles with Scallion-Infused Oil

The combination of scallion-infused oil, soy sauce, and pepper flakes makes this simple noodle dish irresistible. The secret is a good infused oil—and that's very simple to make (see page 11).

1. Bring a pot of water to a boil and cook the noodles according to the package instructions until tender, 3 to 4 minutes. Drain, then rinse the noodles under cold water to prevent them from cooking further, until they are cold to the touch. Set aside to drain well.

2. Heat the infused oil in a medium frying pan over medium heat. Add the garlic and cook until browned, 3 to 4 minutes. Add the soy sauce, gochugaru, sugar, and salt. Cook for about 2 minutes until the sugar dissolves and the sauce begins to simmer.

3. Add the noodles to the sauce. Cook for 1 minute, stirring until the noodles are well coated and hot.

4. Garnish with the sliced scallion and serve.

SERVES 1

3 ounces (90 g) fresh wheat noodles (such as ramen)

¼ cup (60 ml) Scallion-Infused Oil (page 11)

3 garlic cloves, coarsely chopped

2 tablespoons light soy sauce

1 tablespoon gochugaru (ground or flakes)

1 tablespoon superfine sugar

Pinch of salt

1 scallion, 1 small leek (green parts only), or a few fresh chives, thinly sliced, for serving

Hokkien Noodles * HOKKIEN MEE

Hokkien mee is a dish made up of slippery Chinese wheat noodles with a dark, sweet, caramelized sauce. I'm warning you: You'll need to use a napkin after every bite!

1. Bring a pot of water to a boil and cook the noodles according to the package instructions until tender, 3 to 4 minutes. Drain, then rinse the noodles under cold water to prevent them from cooking further, until they are cold to the touch. Set aside to drain well.

2. Heat the oil in a large frying pan over medium heat. Add the tofu and sauté, turning the cubes occasionally, until golden. Add the garlic, bok choy, noodles, vegetable dashi, light soy sauce, dark soy sauce, "fish" sauce, sugar, and cornstarch slurry. Simmer until the sauce thickens. Remove from the heat and transfer to a large serving bowl.

3. In a small bowl, combine the chiles, garlic, lime juice, salt, and sugar. Mix well.

4. Serve the sauce alongside the sautéed noodles.

SERVES 2

10 ounces (283 g) Chinese wheat (chow mein) noodles

2 tablespoons vegetable oil or other neutral oil

Half a 14-ounce (397 g) block firm tofu, pressed and cubed

3 garlic cloves, minced

1 small head bok choy, leaves separated

¾ cup (180 ml) plus 1½ tablespoons Vegetable Dashi (page 12) or vegetable broth

1 tablespoon light soy sauce

1 tablespoon dark soy sauce

2 teaspoons "Fish" Sauce (page 19)

1 teaspoon superfine sugar

1 teaspoon cornstarch mixed with 2 teaspoons water to make a slurry

CHILE SAUCE

2 small red chile peppers, minced

1 garlic clove, minced

1 tablespoon fresh lime juice

1 teaspoon salt

1 teaspoon superfine sugar

SAUTÉED NOODLES

Mixed Vegetables with Glass Noodles * JAPCHAE

Japchae (잡채) means "mixed vegetables." Aside from the vegetables, the principal ingredient in this dish is dangmyeon (당면), Korean noodles made from sweet potatoes, also known as glass noodles. Japchae are simply sweet potato noodles sautéed with vegetables and a protein. It's one of the most popular dishes in Korea. If someone asks me to recommend a good meal to make for company, I don't hesitate to answer "japchae," for the simple reason that everyone loves it. It's hard not to be tempted by these soft, slightly sweet noodles and the irresistible sesame flavor.

1. In a small bowl, combine the soy sauce, sugar, garlic, sesame oil, sesame seeds, and a few grinds of black pepper. Mix until the sugar has dissolved.

2. Bring a large pot of water to a boil and cook the noodles according to the package instructions until they are translucent, about 8 minutes. Remove the noodles from the pot with a slotted spoon and place them in a sieve. (Do not empty the water from the pot.) Rinse the noodles under cold water to prevent them from cooking further, until they are cold to the touch. Drain well, then transfer to a bowl. Cut into shorter lengths with a pair of kitchen shears. Add 3 tablespoons of the sauce and mix well.

3. Fill a large bowl with cold water. Add the spinach to the pot of boiling water. Blanch for 1 minute, then immediately drain and transfer to the cold water to stop the cooking. When cold, drain well, then chop coarsely.

4. Heat the vegetable oil in a medium frying pan over medium heat. Add the carrot, bell pepper, and salt. Sauté until the vegetables begin to soften, then push them to the side of the pan. Add the onion and cook until it becomes translucent. Add the shiitake mushrooms and stir to combine. Cook for another 3 minutes.

5. Add the spinach, noodles, and the remaining sauce. Sauté for 1 to 2 minutes, mixing well. Remove from the heat and transfer to a serving bowl. Garnish with the sliced scallion, sprinkle with sesame seeds, and serve.

SERVES 1

SAUCE

1 tablespoon light soy sauce

1 tablespoon superfine sugar or brown sugar

1 tablespoon minced garlic

1 tablespoon toasted sesame oil

1 teaspoon toasted sesame seeds

Freshly ground black pepper

3.5 ounces (100 g) dangmyeon noodles

3⅓ cups (100 g) fresh spinach

2 tablespoons vegetable oil or other neutral oil

½ carrot, peeled and cut into matchsticks

1 red bell pepper, seeded and cut into matchsticks

Pinch of salt

1 white onion, thinly sliced

4 or 5 fresh shiitake mushrooms, stems removed, thinly sliced

1 scallion, 1 small leek (white and green parts), or 1 small bunch fresh chives, finely chopped, for serving

Sesame seeds, for serving

Drunken Noodles * PAD KEE MAO

If you like Thai cuisine, you probably know drunken noodles, also called pad kee mao. There are a few theories on the origin of the name, but the one I like best is also the simplest: These noodles are perfect after a night of indulgence.

1. Bring a pot of water to a boil and cook the noodles according to the package instructions until tender, about 5 minutes. Drain, then rinse the noodles under cold water to prevent them from cooking further, until they are cold to the touch. Set aside to drain well.

2. In a small bowl, combine the brown sugar, light soy sauce, dark soy sauce, Shaoxing wine, garlic, sesame oil, ginger, shallot, chopped scallion, and chile. Stir well.

3. Heat the vegetable oil in a frying pan over medium heat and add the onion. Cook until translucent, then add the carrot, and bell pepper. Cook for 3 or 4 minutes, then pour in the sauce, most of the scallions, and noodles; mix well to incorporate. Sauté for 1 minute, until the noodles are heated through.

4. Remove from the heat and transfer to a serving bowl. Place the scallion strips on top. Serve warm with lime wedges.

SERVES 1

3.5 ounces (100 g) wide rice noodles

SAUCE

1 tablespoon brown sugar

1 tablespoon light soy sauce

1 tablespoon dark soy sauce

1 tablespoon Shaoxing wine, sherry, rice vinegar, sake, or mirin

3 garlic cloves, coarsely chopped

3 tablespoons sesame oil

1 teaspoon minced fresh ginger

1 shallot, coarsely chopped

1 scallion, 1 small leek (white and green parts), or 1 small bunch fresh chives, chopped, plus 1 scallion (green parts only), cut into 1½-inch (4 cm) lengths, for serving

1 red Thai chile pepper (bird's eye chile), minced

3 tablespoons vegetable oil or other neutral oil

1 small onion, finely chopped

½ carrot, peeled and cut into matchsticks

½ green bell pepper, seeded and cut into matchsticks

1 or 2 lime wedges, for serving

Hakka Noodles

Hakka noodles are a popular Indo-Chinese dish. The name refers to the Hakka people of China, but with Bengal just next door, this recipe is a culinary fusion, incorporating the flavors from nearby Kolkata. The result is the dish we know as Hakka noodles. This is my vegan version, chock-full of vegetables. It's easy to make and delicious.

1. To make the spicy oil, heat the oil in a saucepan over high heat. When the oil is barely smoking, add the crushed chiles and salt. Turn off the heat and cover. Allow the oil to cool to room temperature. Strain into a small glass preserving jar. (Discard the bits of chile.)

2. Bring a pot of water to a boil and cook the noodles according to the package instructions until tender, 3 to 4 minutes. Drain, then rinse the noodles under cold water to prevent them from cooking further, until they are cold to the touch. Set aside to drain well.

3. Heat the vegetable oil in a wok. When the oil is barely smoking, add the scallions, garlic, and minced chiles. Stir-fry for a few seconds, then add the carrots, cabbage, bell pepper, and mushrooms. Stir-fry over high heat for 3 to 4 minutes, until the vegetables are just tender.

4. Add the noodles, soy sauce, 2 tablespoons of the spicy oil, and salt and pepper to taste. Toss to coat and serve!

SERVES 2

SPICY OIL

½ cup (120 ml) vegetable oil or other neutral oil

5 dried red Thai chile peppers (bird's eye chile), crushed

1 teaspoon salt

8 ounces (227 g) somyeon (thin wheat) noodles

2 tablespoons vegetable oil or other neutral oil

5 scallions, 3 small leeks (white and green parts), or 1 large bunch fresh chives, chopped

1 garlic clove, minced

2 dried red chile peppers, minced

2 medium carrots, peeled and cut into matchsticks

1 cup (80 g) shredded white cabbage

1 small green bell pepper, seeded and cut into matchsticks

7 medium white button mushrooms, thinly sliced

2 tablespoons light soy sauce

Salt and freshly ground black pepper

(Tip:) You can store any remaining spicy oil, tightly capped, in the refrigerator for a few days.

Yaki Udon

Yaki udon is a Japanese sautéed noodle dish traditionally made with meat, crunchy vegetables, and a delicious soy-based sauce. Yaki translates as "grilled," but the ingredients are actually sautéed. If you go to an izakaya (a bar or pub) in Japan, you'll often see yaki udon on the menu because it's a very popular dish.

1. In a small bowl, combine the "oyster" sauce, dark soy sauce, light soy sauce, mirin, sugar, and sriracha. Stir well.

2. Heat the oil in a wok or frying pan over medium heat. Add the scallions and garlic and cook for 1 minute. Add the mushrooms and bok choy. Stir and cook until the vegetables are tender.

3. Add the noodles and the sauce, and mix to coat the noodles well. Cook without stirring, so the noodles turn lightly golden. Divide between two bowls, sprinkle with the sliced scallion, and enjoy while hot.

SERVES 2

SAUCE

2 tablespoons "Oyster" Sauce (page 18)

1 tablespoon dark soy sauce

1 tablespoon light soy sauce

1 tablespoon mirin

1 tablespoon superfine sugar

1 tablespoon sriracha

¼ cup (60 ml) vegetable oil or other neutral oil

4 scallions, 2 small leeks (white and green parts), or 1 large bunch fresh chives, coarsely chopped, plus 1 scallion (green parts only), thinly sliced, for serving

4 garlic cloves, minced

5 fresh shiitake mushrooms, stems removed, coarsely chopped

2 small heads bok choy, leaves separated

8 ounces (227 g) Homemade Udon Noodles (page 20) or store-bought fresh udon, cooked

SAUTÉED NOODLES

Pad Thai

Pad thai is a traditional stir-fried noodle dish in Thailand. These days, it's available everywhere—you can even buy it from food trucks. The key to a good pad thai recipe is striking the perfect balance between the sweet, salty, tart, and spicy flavors. You'll find this balance by using soy sauce, coconut sugar, and lime juice.

1. Bring a pot of water to a boil and cook the noodles according to the package instructions until they are al dente, 2 to 3 minutes. (They will finish cooking in the sauce later.) Drain, then rinse the noodles under cold water to prevent them from cooking further, until they are cold to the touch. Set aside to drain well.

2. Heat the oil in large frying pan over medium heat. Add the seitan and cook, stirring often, 2 to 3 minutes, until lightly browned.

3. Move the seitan to the edge of the frying pan and add the noodles, soy sauce, coconut sugar, and a splash of lime juice.

4. Add enough water to the pan to prevent the noodles from sticking (about ¼ cup/60 ml), and cook until the liquid has evaporated. Add the bean sprouts, carrot, garlic, and chopped scallions. Stir-fry until the vegetables are cooked.

5. Serve topped with the peanuts, lime quarters, and sliced scallion, and the cilantro, tomato, cucumber, and more bean sprouts, if using.

SERVES 2

- 8 ounces (227 g) rice noodles
- 4 tablespoons vegetable oil or other neutral oil
- 10 strips seitan or half a 14-ounce (397 g) block firm tofu, pressed and cut into ½-inch (1.25 cm) slices
- ¼ cup (60 ml) plus 1 tablespoon light soy sauce
- 2 tablespoons coconut sugar or maple syrup
- Juice of 1 lime
- 1 cup (100 g) fresh bean spouts, plus more for serving (optional)
- ½ medium carrot, peeled and cut into matchsticks
- 1 garlic clove, coarsely chopped
- 1 small bunch scallions (white and green parts), chopped

GARNISH

- 3 tablespoons crushed peanuts
- 1 lime, quartered
- 1 scallion (green parts only), thinly sliced
- Fresh cilantro sprigs (optional)
- ½ small plum tomato, quartered (optional)
- A few slices of English cucumber (optional)

(Tip:) Pad thai has the best flavor when served straight from the pan!

Hot Noodle
Soups

Toshikoshi Soba

On New Year's Eve in Japan, it's customary to reflect on the year past and welcome the year to come, while eating a bowl of warm soba noodles called toshikoshi soba (年越し蕎麦). According to tradition, toshikoshi soba is generally served in its most simple version: buckwheat soba noodles in a hot dashi broth, garnished only with scallions.

1. The night before serving, put the kombu in a jar with 3 cups (720 ml) water, cover, and leave to soak overnight.

2. The next day, transfer the kombu and its soaking water to a saucepan. Over low heat, bring the water to a boil. Turn off the heat and remove the kombu. (Reserve the kombu for another use, if desired.) Allow the broth to rest for about 10 minutes.

3. Add the sake, mirin, soy sauce, salt, and mushrooms to the broth. Return to the heat and bring to a boil. Cook for about 5 minutes. Remove from the heat and cover.

4. To prepare the garnishes, in a medium bowl, submerge the wakame in enough water to completely cover. Allow to rehydrate until soft, then drain. Cut the inari in half on the diagonal. Grate the daikon, then squeeze and press it into 2 balls; set aside on a small plate. Punch through the carrot coins with a flower-shaped food cutter. Carve a star pattern in the tops of the mushrooms.

5. Bring a pot of water to a boil and cook the noodles according to the package instructions until tender, about 5 minutes. Drain, then rinse under cold water to prevent the noodles from cooking further, until they are cold to the touch. Drain well. Divide equally between two bowls.

6. To make the tempura, line a large plate with paper towels. Thinly slice the squash. In a bowl, mix the rice flour, all-purpose flour, cornstarch, salt, and baking soda. Add sparkling water a little at a time, mixing well, until it forms a batter with the consistency of heavy cream. Fill a deep saucepan about halfway with oil and heat over medium-high heat until it reaches 350°F (180°C); if you don't have a cooking thermometer, test the heat by dropping a pinch of the batter into the oil. If it sizzles, the oil is ready. Using tongs, dip a few slices of squash in the batter to coat them completely, then gently lower them into the oil. Fry for 3 to 4 minutes, until golden. Remove them with a slotted spoon and transfer to the prepared plate. Let the oil return to 350°F (180°C) before repeating with the remaining squash slices.

7. Strain the broth into a clean saucepan and bring it almost to a boil over medium-high heat. (Reserve the mushrooms for another use, if desired.) Pour the hot broth over the soba noodles. Garnish each bowl of noodles with half an inari, a few pieces of tempura squash, a shiitake mushroom, half of the wakame, 1 radish ball, 2 or 3 carrot flowers, and half of the sliced scallion. Serve hot. (You can serve the extra tempura on the side.)

SERVES 2

BROTH

1 sheet kombu

1 tablespoon sake

1 tablespoon mirin

2 tablespoons light soy sauce

1 tablespoon coarse salt

2 dried shiitake mushrooms, stems removed

GARNISHES

2 tablespoons dried wakame

1 piece store-bought inari (rice-stuffed fried tofu)

One 2-inch (5 cm) piece daikon radish

4 to 6 carrot coins, ⅛-inch (3 mm) thick

2 fresh shiitake mushrooms, stems removed

1 scallion (green parts only), thinly sliced

8 ounces (227 g) soba (buckwheat) noodles

TEMPURA

½ small butternut or 1 honeynut squash, peeled and seeded, or 1 medium sweet potato, peeled

⅓ cup (60 g) sweet rice flour

½ cup (60 g) all-purpose flour

1½ tablespoons cornstarch

Pinch of salt

1 tablespoon baking soda

½ cup (120 ml) sparkling water, or more or less as needed

Vegetable oil or other neutral oil, for frying

Vietnamese Pho

Along with banh mi, pho is the most popular Vietnamese dish. It's a soup that transforms affordable, easily accessible ingredients into a delicious meal. It's as easy to make pho as other soups, but it's worth paying particular attention to the broth and its spices and aromatics. Browning the ginger and onion over high heat intensifies the flavor. In this vegan pho, the broth is flavorful, light, and rich with spices. Served with rice noodles, this recipe is naturally gluten-free.

1. To make the broth, heat the oil in a large saucepan over high heat. Add the onions and ginger and cook until they are well browned but not burned. Add the coriander, star anise, cinnamon, and peppercorns, and cook until fragrant. Add 2 quarts (2 L) water, the carrots, turnip, soy sauce, salt, and sugar. Bring to a boil, then lower the heat and simmer for 1 hour.

2. Strain the broth into a clean pot. (Discard the solids.) Adjust the seasoning with salt and sugar, if necessary. Keep warm over low heat.

3. Bring a large pot of water to a boil. Fill a large bowl with ice and water. Add the bok choy to the boiling water and cook for 3 minutes, until barely tender. Remove the bok choy from the boiling water using a slotted spoon and immediately shock it in the ice water for 1 minute or until cool. Remove from the ice water with the slotted spoon and drain well.

4. In the same pot of boiling water, cook the noodles according to the package instructions until tender, about 5 minutes. Drain well.

5. To assemble, divide the noodles among five deep soup bowls. To each bowl, add the broth, 3 slices of the tofu, a few bok choy leaves, a few cilantro, mint, and basil sprigs, some bean sprouts, jalapeño slices, and a lime wedge. To serve, let each person add sriracha to taste. (In my opinion, sriracha is essential!)

SERVES 5

BROTH

¼ cup (60 ml) vegetable oil or other neutral oil

2 white onions, coarsely chopped

One 3-inch (7.5 cm) piece fresh ginger, peeled and thinly sliced

2 tablespoons coriander seeds

2 star anise

1 cinnamon stick

1 tablespoon black peppercorns

2 medium carrots, coarsely chopped

1 white turnip, coarsely chopped

¼ cup (60 ml) plus 1 tablespoon light soy sauce

3 tablespoons fine salt

3 tablespoons superfine sugar

4 small heads bok choy, leaves separated

1 pound (16 oz/454 g) flat, thick rice noodles

One 14-ounce (397 g) block firm tofu, cut into 15 slices

GARNISH

Fresh cilantro sprigs

Fresh mint sprigs

Fresh Thai basil sprigs

Fresh bean sprouts

2 jalapeño chiles, thinly sliced

1 lime, cut into 5 wedges

Sriracha (optional)

HOT NOODLE SOUPS

Miso Ramen

Miso ramen is a Japanese noodle soup flavored with miso. It's the most popular ramen in Japan, even though there are a million variations. Miso is made from fermented soybeans and has a strong umami flavor: It's the secret to adding depth and flavor to the soup. For this recipe I use white miso, which is not as intense as the darker varieties.

1. Heat a medium saucepan over medium heat. Add 1 tablespoon of the oil, the tofu, and dark soy sauce. Cook for 4 to 5 minutes, stirring occasionally to prevent sticking, until the tofu is well browned. Remove from the heat, pour into a bowl, and set aside to cool.

2. In the same saucepan, cook the mushrooms in the remaining oil until they are golden and tender. Add the shallots, garlic, and ginger, and cook for 2 to 3 minutes, stirring occasionally.

3. Stir in the miso, light soy sauce, rice vinegar, and spicy oil. Add the vegetable dashi and bring to a boil. Lower the heat and simmer gently for 20 minutes.

4. Bring a pot of water to a boil and cook the noodles according to the package instructions until tender, about 2 minutes. Drain the noodles. Divide them equally between two bowls.

5. Ladle the broth over each bowl of noodles, making sure to scoop up some mushrooms. Garnish each bowl with half the tofu, the corn, sliced scallions, and sesame seeds. Add a splash of spicy oil, if you like an extra kick, and serve.

SERVES 2

2 tablespoons vegetable oil or other neutral oil

Half a 14-ounce (397 g) block soft or firm tofu, pressed and crumbled

1 tablespoon dark soy sauce

7 fresh shiitake mushrooms, stems removed, thinly sliced

2 shallots, chopped

3 garlic cloves, minced

One ½- to ¾-inch (1.25 to 2 cm) piece fresh ginger, grated

2 tablespoons white miso

2 tablespoons light soy sauce

1 tablespoon rice vinegar

2 tablespoons Spicy Oil Infused with Garlic, Gochugaru, and Sesame Seeds (page 10) or store-bought chili crisp, plus more for serving (optional)

1 quart (1 L) Vegetable Dashi (page 12) or vegetable broth

8 ounces (227 g) rice noodles or ramen noodles

GARNISH

¼ cup (45 g) cooked corn kernels

3 scallions, 2 small leeks (green parts only), or 1 bunch fresh chives, thinly sliced

2 tablespoons toasted sesame seeds

Shoyu Ramen

Shoyu ramen is a ramen noodle dish flavored with shoyu, the Japanese word for soy sauce. Shoyu ramen uses one of the four types of tare (seasonings) to enhance a broth, the three others being Miso Ramen (page 80), shio ramen (ramen with salt), and tonkotsu ramen, which is made with pork-bone stock and a garnish of fried pork cutlet.

1. To make the broth, bring 2 cups (480 ml) water and the kombu to a boil over low heat. Remove from the heat and allow to sit, covered, for 5 minutes, then strain into a small bowl. (Reserve the kombu for another use, if desired.)

2. In a saucepan, combine the broth and vegetable dashi. Heat over low heat for 2 to 3 minutes, then add the shiitake, button, and enoki mushrooms and cook until tender.

3. To make the shoyu seasoning, heat a frying pan over medium heat. Add the sesame oil, garlic, and ginger, and cook for about 30 seconds, until browned. Stir in the soy sauce and mirin, then remove from the heat. Add the shoyu seasoning to the broth a spoonful at a time, until the broth is seasoned to your taste.

4. Bring a pot of water to a boil and cook the noodles according to the package instructions until al dente, 30 seconds to 1 minute. (They will finish cooking in the broth later.) Drain, then divide equally between two bowls.

5. Place about 1 teaspoon toasted sesame oil and the vegan "chicken" in a frying pan and cook according to the package instructions, until golden and crispy.

6. Pour the broth equally over the two bowls of noodles. Add the mushrooms, the vegan "chicken," the sliced scallions, and a drizzle of sesame oil. Sprinkle with the togarashi or add a drizzle of spicy oil, if desired. Add 2 pieces of nori on the edge of each bowl just before serving.

SERVES 2

BROTH AND MUSHROOMS

1 sheet kombu

2 cups (480 ml) Vegetable Dashi (page 12) or vegetable broth

2 fresh shiitake mushrooms, stems removed, thinly sliced

4 white button mushrooms, thinly sliced

1¼ cups (80 g) enoki mushrooms

SHOYU SEASONING

1 tablespoon toasted sesame oil

2 garlic cloves, grated

2 teaspoons grated fresh ginger

3 tablespoons light soy sauce

1 tablespoon mirin

7 ounces (200 g) ramen noodles

GARNISH

Toasted sesame oil

8 pieces store-bought vegan "chicken" (not nuggets or breaded)

2 scallions, 1 small leek (green parts only), or 1 small bunch fresh chives, sliced

Shichimi togarashi or Spicy Oil Infused with Garlic, Gochugaru, and Sesame Seeds (page 10) or store-bought chili crisp (optional)

1 sheet nori seaweed, quartered

Tip: Store any leftover shoyu seasoning in a tightly capped bottle or small glass preserving jar in the refrigerator for up to 3 days.

20-Minute Ramen

Sometimes I like to keep things simple, so I cook with only a handful of ingredients—that's all you'll need for this comforting, texture-rich, and incredibly quick ramen.

1. Combine 1 cup (240 ml) of the vegetable dashi, the ginger, and garlic in a small saucepan over medium heat. Bring to a boil and cook for 5 minutes.

2. In a small bowl, whisk together the remaining dashi and the miso until smooth. Add the miso mixture, the parsley, soy sauce, salt, and scallions to the saucepan. Mix well and bring to a boil. Cook until the scallions are soft, about 5 minutes.

3. Add the noodles to the saucepan and cook until they are soft, about 3 minutes.

4. Pour into a deep bowl and sprinkle with the chives and sesame seeds. Drizzle with a little spicy oil for an extra kick, if desired, before eating.

SERVES 1

2 cups (480 ml) Vegetable Dashi (page 12) or vegetable broth

One ½- to ¾-inch (1.25 to 2 cm) piece fresh ginger, grated

2 garlic cloves, coarsely chopped

1 tablespoon white miso

A few fresh parsley leaves

1 tablespoon light soy sauce

1 teaspoon fine salt

¼ cup (22 g) plus 1 tablespoon finely chopped scallion, leek (white and green parts), or fresh chives

3.5 ounces (100 g) rice noodles or instant ramen noodles

GARNISH

1 small bunch fresh chives, 1 scallion, or 1 small leek (green parts only), finely chopped

Sesame seeds

Spicy Oil Infused with Garlic, Gochugaru, and Sesame Seeds (page 10) or store-bought chili crisp (optional)

Kitsune Udon

Kitsune means "fox" in Japanese, and tradition says that Inari Ōkami, the Shinto deity of fertility, prosperity, and agriculture had an army of foxes as servants. Legend has it that these foxes loved aburaage, or fried tofu, which is why most of the dishes containing it have the words inari or kitsune in their name. In the case of kitsune udon, the dish is made up of a rich broth, udon noodles, and fried tofu seasoned with soy sauce, sake, and sugar.

1. In a saucepan, combine the vegetable dashi, soy sauce, mirin, and salt. Bring to a boil, then lower the heat and simmer for about 15 minutes. Cover and cook an additional 5 minutes. Adjust the seasonings to taste.

2. Bring a small pot of water to a boil and cook the aburaage for 2 to 3 minutes. Add the soy sauce, sake, mirin, and sugar, and simmer for 10 minutes. Drain the aburaage and cut each piece in half on the diagonal, to make four triangles.

3. Bring another pot of water to a boil and cook the noodles according to the package instructions until tender, 2 to 5 minutes. (Or follow the directions on page 20 if you are using homemade udon noodles.) Drain the noodles and divide them equally between two bowls.

4. Pour the broth equally over the two bowls of noodles, and garnish with the aburaage, carrots, and sliced scallions. Serve immediately.

SERVES 2

BROTH

3⅓ cups (800 ml) Vegetable Dashi (page 12) or vegetable broth

2 tablespoons light soy sauce

2 tablespoons mirin

½ teaspoon salt

2 store-bought frozen aburaage (fried tofu shells), defrosted

1 teaspoon light soy sauce

1 teaspoon sake

1 tablespoon mirin

1 tablespoon superfine sugar

10.5 ounces (300 g) store-bought fresh udon or Homemade Udon Noodles (page 20)

GARNISH

6 to 8 carrot coins, a scant ¼ inch (6 mm) thick, punched through with a flower-shaped cutter

2 scallions (white and green parts), finely chopped

HOT NOODLE SOUPS

Curry Udon

This curry udon recipe is the perfect combination of udon soup and Japanese katsu curry. The key ingredient in this dish is the Japanese curry cube. It adds depth and a rich and spicy flavor to the broth, and that's exactly what we're aiming for. You can also add a vegan katsu (cutlet), if you like.

1. If making the vegan katsu, prepare three shallow bowls: One with ½ cup (120 ml) water, a second with the flour, and a third with the panko. Line a large plate with paper towels. Dip each zucchini strip in the water, then the flour. Repeat two more times per strip, until well coated. Then dip the strips in the water, then the panko, and repeat two more times per strip. Set the strips aside on a wire rack until all are fully coated. Heat about ¼ inch (6 mm) oil in a frying pan over medium heat. Add the zucchini strips and fry, turning them once or twice, until they're golden and crispy on both sides. Place the zucchini katsu on the prepared plate to drain.

2. Line another plate with paper towels. In a frying pan, cook the vegan "chicken" in about 1 teaspoon oil, according to the package instructions, until golden. (If you made the katsu, cook the "chicken" in the same pan in the remaining oil. You can add a bit more oil to the pan, if needed.) Place the "chicken" on the prepared plate.

3. To make the broth, add the onion to the oil in the frying pan (if there is less than 2 tablespoons oil, add more) and cook until translucent. Add the vegetable dashi and carrot, if using, bring to a boil, and cook until the carrot is tender. Add the noodles and cook for 2 minutes, until the noodles are heated through. Gradually add the curry cube to the broth, stirring gently until the curry cube dissolves and the broth thickens. Add the "chicken" and scallion-infused oil and stir.

4. Divide the noodles, carrots, "chicken," and broth equally between two bowls. Top with the katsu, if using. Garnish with the chopped scallion, and serve hot.

SERVES 2

VEGAN KATSU (OPTIONAL) AND "CHICKEN"

¾ cup (100 g) all-purpose flour

1¾ cups (100 g) panko or bread crumbs

1 medium zucchini, cut lengthwise into ¼-inch (6 mm) slices

Vegetable oil or other neutral oil, for frying

8 to 10 pieces store-bought vegan "chicken" (not nuggets or breaded), cut in half

BROTH AND UDON

1 yellow onion, chopped

2 tablespoons vegetable oil or other neutral oil

2½ cups (600 ml) Vegetable Dashi (page 12) or vegetable broth

1 carrot, peeled and coarsely chopped (optional)

8 ounces (227 g) Homemade Udon Noodles (page 20) or store-bought fresh udon, cooked

½ Japanese curry cube (such as S&B Golden Curry Japanese Curry Mix), crumbled

3 tablespoons Scallion-Infused Oil (page 11)

1 scallion, 1 small leek (white and green parts), or 1 small bunch chives, chopped, for serving

Laksa

Laksa is a spicy coconut noodle soup that has an amazing aroma and is rich in flavors. This colorful, nutritious, filling, and scrumptious dish is a staple of Malaysian cuisine, and is also popular in Singapore. It's essential to make your own laksa seasoning paste. It'll be worth it in the end, and you'll get a taste of the real thing.

1. To make the laksa seasoning, combine the shallots, garlic, lemongrass, turmeric, ginger, chiles, nori, cashews, and cilantro in a food processor. Blend until the mixture becomes a paste, at least 30 seconds. Heat the oil in a deep frying pan over low heat. Add the paste and cook until lightly brown, stirring often, about 10 minutes. Add the coriander, cumin, and paprika, then cook for about 3 minutes.

2. Add the vegetable dashi to the laksa seasoning. Bring to a boil, turn down the heat, and simmer for 30 minutes. Add the coconut milk, brown sugar, lime juice, and salt, then simmer for 2 to 3 minutes. Adjust the seasonings to taste.

3. While the broth is simmering, steam the carrot and the broccoli and mushrooms (if using). Place them in a microwave-safe container with 1 tablespoon water. Cover and cook in the microwave until the vegetables are soft, about 5 minutes.

4. Bring a pot of water to a boil. Cook the noodles according to the package instructions until tender, about 5 minutes, then drain.

5. Add the steamed vegetables to the broth and cook for 5 minutes.

6. Divide the broth and vegetables equally between two bowls. Add an equal portion of noodles to each bowl. Garnish with a few bean sprouts, the cilantro leaves, chopped chile, a lime wedge, and the tofu (if using), and serve.

SERVES 2

LAKSA SEASONING

2 medium shallots, chopped

4 garlic cloves, minced

1 stalk lemongrass (white part only), finely chopped

One ¾-inch (2 cm) piece fresh turmeric, chopped, or 1 teaspoon ground turmeric

One 1½-inch (4 cm) piece fresh ginger, chopped

3 red chile peppers, minced

2 tablespoons crumbled nori seaweed

¾ cup (70 g) roasted unsalted cashews

1 handful of fresh cilantro sprigs

2 to 3 tablespoons vegetable oil or other neutral oil

1 tablespoon ground coriander

1 tablespoon ground cumin

2 teaspoons sweet paprika

BROTH

2 cups (480 ml) Vegetable Dashi (page 12) or vegetable broth

¾ cup (180 ml) coconut milk

1 tablespoon brown sugar

Juice of 1 lime

1 teaspoon salt

½ medium carrot, peeled and coarsely chopped

6 broccoli florets (optional)

6 cremini mushrooms (optional)

8 ounces (227 g) thick, flat rice noodles

GARNISH

2 small handfuls of bean sprouts

Leaves from ½ small bunch fresh cilantro

1 red chile pepper, chopped

2 lime wedges

Half a 14-ounce (397 g) block soft or firm tofu, cubed (optional)

Misua Soup

Misua are very thin noodles made from wheat flour and salt, that originated in Fujian, China. In Chinese culture, misua means long life, making this a traditional birthday dish. The noodles are generally served with eggs, oysters, shiitake mushrooms, meat, scallions, and toasted nuts.

1. To prepare the tofu, line a large plate with paper towels. Heat the oil in a large, deep frying pan over medium-high heat. Add the tofu and cook until golden on all sides. Remove the tofu from the pan with a slotted spoon and transfer to the prepared plate to drain.

2. To make the fried garlic, add the ¼ cup (60 ml) oil to the oil remaining in the pan used to fry the tofu. Add the garlic and salt and cook over medium heat, stirring frequently, just until the garlic becomes crunchy and golden brown. (Don't let it burn, or it will become bitter.) Transfer the garlic to the prepared plate, leaving the oil in the pan.

3. Sauté the onion and tomato in the pan until caramelized. Add the vegetable dashi and the bok choy, and simmer for 5 minutes.

4. Add the tofu, "oyster" sauce, and noodles, and simmer for 5 minutes, until the noodles are tender. Season with salt and pepper.

5. Divide between two bowls. Before you dig in, top with the fried garlic and spicy oil and the chopped peanuts, if using.

SERVES 2

TOFU

2 tablespoons vegetable oil or other neutral oil

Half a 14-ounce (397 g) block firm tofu, pressed and cubed

FRIED GARLIC

¼ cup (60 ml) vegetable oil or other neutral oil

6 garlic cloves, coarsely chopped

½ teaspoon fine salt

1 yellow onion, chopped

1 small plum tomato, finely diced

2½ cups (600 ml) Vegetable Dashi (page 12) or vegetable broth

2 small heads bok choy, quartered lengthwise

1 tablespoon "Oyster" Sauce (page 18)

8 ounces (227 g) misua noodles or angel hair pasta

Salt and freshly ground black pepper

GARNISH

2 tablespoons Spicy Oil Infused with Garlic, Gochugaru, and Sesame Seeds (page 10) or store-bought chili crisp

2 tablespoons chopped peanuts (optional)

Creamy Coconut-Curry Ramen

You only need a few simple ingredients and 20 minutes to make this recipe. The curry-infused coconut cream is just divine and gives the broth depth. This dish is warm and filled with spice—but not too much.

1. Heat the sesame oil in a large, deep frying pan over medium heat. Add the garlic, scallions, and carrot, and cook until browned, 5 minutes. Add the onion powder, garlic powder, ginger, curry powder, turmeric, paprika, salt, pepper, and curry paste. Cook for 2 to 3 minutes, until fragrant, then pour the lime juice into the frying pan and scrape up the brown bits to incorporate them into the juice.

2. Stir in the vegetable dashi and coconut cream. Bring to a boil, then lower the heat and simmer for 10 minutes.

3. Stir in the cornstarch slurry and simmer until the soup thickens.

4. Add the noodles to the soup and cook for 5 minutes, until tender, then divide equally between three bowls. To serve, sprinkle with the cilantro, and top with 2 or 3 slices tofu and the chopped scallion, if using.

SERVES 3

- 3 tablespoons toasted sesame oil
- 8 garlic cloves, minced
- 4 scallions, 2 small leeks (white and green parts), or 1 bunch chives, finely chopped
- 1 carrot, peeled and thinly sliced
- 2 teaspoons onion powder
- 1 teaspoon garlic powder
- ½ teaspoon ground ginger
- 1½ teaspoons curry powder
- 1 teaspoon ground turmeric
- 1 teaspoon sweet paprika
- 1 teaspoon fine salt
- 1 teaspoon freshly ground black pepper
- 1 teaspoon Thai green curry paste
- Juice of 1 lime
- 1 quart (1 L) Vegetable Dashi (page 12) or vegetable broth
- One 13.5 ounce (400 ml) can coconut cream
- 2 tablespoons cornstarch, mixed with 2 tablespoons water to make a slurry
- 9 ounces (255 g) wheat noodles (such as ramen)

GARNISH

- Fresh cilantro leaves, chopped
- 6 to 9 small square slices soft tofu (optional)
- 1 scallion (white and green parts), finely chopped (optional)

HOT NOODLE SOUPS

The Ultimate Mushroom Ramen

Making ramen can be very simple, but the best ramen is a bit more complex. It starts with a good broth, and a variety of ingredients. Dried shiitake mushrooms add a strong earthy flavor, the dried porcini mushrooms give it a deep umami flavor, the enoki add a unique sweetness, and the sun-dried tomatoes highlight the vegetable flavor—not to mention the toppings, which perfectly complement the whole dish.

1. The night before, in a large bowl, combine the kombu, shiitake, porcini, sun-dried tomatoes, and soybeans. Cover with enough water to completely submerge the vegetables, cover, and leave to soak overnight.

2. The next day, drain the vegetables and transfer them to a large saucepan. Add 1 quart (1 L) water, the cabbage, bell pepper, enoki, cremini, and onion. Bring to a boil, then immediately remove the kombu (reserve for another use, if desired). Turn the heat down to low, cover, and simmer for 2 hours.

3. Strain the broth into a clean saucepan. Remove the mushrooms and set them aside in a bowl. Set aside the tomatoes in another bowl. Discard the soybeans (or reserve for another use, if desired).

4. In a small frying pan, combine the maple syrup, mirin, sake, 2 tablespoons of the soy sauce, the sugar, salt, and miso. Bring to a boil over medium heat, then cook for 3 minutes. Remove from the heat and gradually add to the broth.

5. Cut the cremini into ¼-inch (6 mm) slices and place in a clean frying pan with the enoki, the sesame oil, and the remaining soy sauce. Cook, stirring occasionally, until golden brown, then remove from the heat.

6. Bring a pot of water to a boil and cook the noodles according to the package instructions until tender, about 2 minutes. Drain, then rinse under cold water to prevent the noodles from cooking further, until they are cold to the touch. Drain well. Divide equally between two deep bowls.

7. Bring the broth to a boil, then remove from the heat. Pour the hot broth over the noodles. Add the sautéed mushrooms, the sun-dried tomatoes, the bamboo shoots, a generous spoonful of spicy oil, and 4 to 6 slices of vegan "chicken" (if using). Top with the chopped scallions. If using, add the nori on the edge of the bowl just before serving.

SERVES 2

- 1 sheet kombu
- 2 dried shiitake mushrooms, stems removed
- 3 dried porcini mushrooms
- 4 sun-dried tomatoes
- 1 tablespoon yellow soybeans
- 4 napa cabbage leaves
- 1 red bell pepper, seeded and cut into strips
- 1½ cups (100 g) enoki mushrooms
- 3 cremini mushrooms
- 1 onion, chopped
- 2 tablespoons maple syrup
- 2 tablespoons mirin
- 1 tablespoon sake
- ¼ cup (60 ml) light soy sauce
- 1 teaspoon brown sugar
- 1 teaspoon fine salt
- 1 tablespoon white miso
- 2 tablespoons toasted sesame oil
- 8 ounces (227 g) wheat noodles (such as ramen)
- A few slices of bamboo shoots (from one 8-ounce/225 g can), drained
- Spicy Oil Infused with Garlic, Gochugaru, and Sesame Seeds (page 10) or store-bought chili crisp
- 8 to 12 pieces store-bought vegan "chicken," cooked according to package instructions (optional)
- 2 scallions, 1 small leek (green parts only), or 1 very small bunch chives, finely chopped
- 1 sheet nori seaweed, torn into large pieces (optional)

More Noodle Recipes

Dandan Noodles

Dandan noodles are one of the best noodle dishes in the world! It's a Chinese street food classic from the Sichuan region that combines astonishing flavors in a simple bowl of noodles.

1. To make the sauce, in a small bowl, combine 1 to 2 tablespoons water with the spicy oil, tahini, soy sauce, sesame oil, black vinegar, Sichuan pepper, and garlic. Mix well.

2. For the garnish, heat the sesame oil in a frying pan over medium heat. Add the mushrooms and shallot and cook, stirring occasionally, until golden brown. Add the soy sauce, Shaoxing wine, and sugar. Simmer for 3 to 5 minutes over low heat.

3. Bring a pot of water to a boil and cook the noodles according to the package instructions until tender, 2 to 5 minutes. Drain, then rinse the noodles under cold water to prevent them from cooking further, until they are cold to the touch. Drain well and transfer to a deep bowl.

4. Pour the sauce over the noodles and add the mushroom garnish. To serve, sprinkle with the chopped scallions. Mix thoroughly before eating.

SERVES 1

SAUCE

3 tablespoons Spicy Oil with Garlic, Gochugaru, and Sesame Seeds (page 10) or store-bought chili crisp

2 teaspoons tahini

2 tablespoons light soy sauce

2 teaspoons toasted sesame oil

1 tablespoon black vinegar

Pinch of ground Sichuan pepper

1 garlic clove, chopped

GARNISH

1 tablespoon toasted sesame oil

6 large mushrooms (such as white button or shiitake), stems removed, finely chopped

1 shallot, finely chopped

1 tablespoon dark soy sauce

2 tablespoons Shaoxing wine, sherry, rice vinegar, black vinegar, sake, or mirin

1 teaspoon superfine sugar

2 scallions, 1 small leek (green parts only), or 1 small bunch chives, finely chopped

3.5 ounces (100 g) wheat noodles (such as ramen)

Biang Biang Noodles

If you've never heard of or tasted biang biang noodles, the name might seem strange. It comes from the sound of the noodle dough hitting the work surface as they are pulled by hand!

1. In a large bowl, combine the flour and the salt. Gradually incorporate ¾ cup (180 ml) water, using chopsticks to stir. Add another tablespoon water, if necessary. Knead in the bowl for 5 minutes, until smooth, then shape into a ball.

2. Allow the dough to rest, covered, in the refrigerator for 45 minutes.

3. Divide the dough into 12 equal pieces. Roll each piece into a ball and coat well with oil. Cover and allow to rest for 30 minutes at room temperature.

4. Working with one dough ball at a time, use a rolling pin to roll the dough into a rectangle, about 8 inches (20 cm) long and 1½ inches (4 cm) wide. Score in the middle, lengthwise, with a chopstick. (You will separate the dough into two pieces later.) Repeat with the remaining pieces of dough.

5. This is the most important step! Bring a large pot of water to a boil and fill a large bowl with ice water. Lift one piece of dough from the work surface. Gently stretch the dough lengthwise, then slap it against the work surface as you stretch it again. Pull the dough apart along the scoring, to separate it into two pieces. Add to the boiling water and cook for 2 to 3 minutes, until they float. Remove the noodles from the pot using a slotted spoon and immerse in the bowl of ice water. Repeat with the remaining dough.

6. Once all of the noodles are cooked, drain off the cold water and divide the noodles equally among four deep bowls. (Do not empty the water from the pot.)

7. Fill the bowl with fresh ice water. In the same pot of boiling water, cook the spinach for about 1 minute or the bok choy for 2 to 3 minutes, until just wilted. Drain, then transfer to the ice water to stop the cooking. Let cool for about 1 minute, then drain well.

8. To make the sauce, heat the oil in a small saucepan over medium heat. Add the garlic, sliced scallions, gochugaru, sesame seeds, soy sauce, and vinegar, and simmer for 1 minute.

9. Divide the sauce between the bowls of noodles and mix well. Add a few spinach or bok choy leaves to each bowl and sprinkle with the sliced scallion. Mix thoroughly before eating.

SERVES 4

NOODLES

3⅓ cups (400 g) all-purpose flour

1 tablespoon salt

Vegetable oil or other neutral oil

GARNISH

1 bunch fresh spinach or 1 small head bok choy, leaves separated

1 scallion, 1 small leek (green parts only), or 1 small bunch chives, thinly sliced

SAUCE

2 tablespoons vegetable oil or other neutral oil

2 garlic cloves, minced

2 scallions, 1 small leek (white and green parts), or 1 small bunch fresh chives, thinly sliced

2 tablespoons ground gochugaru

1 tablespoon sesame seeds

2 tablespoons light soy sauce

2 tablespoons rice vinegar

MORE NOODLE RECIPES

Somen with Artichokes and Miso Butter

The idea for this somen noodle dish came to me a few years ago when I found a can of artichoke bottoms in my cupboard. As a child, I always ate artichokes with vinaigrette, but I created this recipe in search of new flavors. I cooked the artichoke bottoms in a miso butter I had prepared the night before. When they began to caramelize, I drizzled lemon juice on top. I loved this dish at first bite.

1. To make the miso butter, in a small bowl, thoroughly mix the butter, miso, garlic, and sriracha until uniform. Set aside ¼ cup (60 g) of the miso butter. Transfer the remaining miso butter to a piece of parchment paper, roll into a sausage shape, and store in the refrigerator.

2. Heat 3 tablespoons of the oil in a frying pan over medium heat. Add the artichoke bottoms and cook until browned on both sides.

3. To the reserved miso butter, add ⅓ cup (80 ml) water, the sugar and soy sauce, and mix well. Pour the mixture over the artichokes, and allow them to slowly caramelize.

4. Bring a pot of water to a boil and cook the noodles according to the package instructions until tender, about 4 minutes. Drain well, then transfer to a deep bowl and mix with the remaining oil.

5. When the artichokes are well caramelized, place them on top of the noodles. Pour the lemon juice into the frying pan and scrape up the brown bits to incorporate them into the juice.

6. To serve, pour the juices from the pan over the noodles and artichokes and sprinkle with the sliced scallions.

SERVES 1

MISO BUTTER

⅔ cup (150 g) unsalted vegan butter, softened

¼ cup (70 g) brown miso

2 garlic cloves, minced

1 tablespoon sriracha

¼ cup (60 ml) vegetable oil or other neutral oil

Half a 14-ounce (397 g) can artichoke bottoms (about 3 pieces), drained well

1 tablespoon superfine sugar

1 tablespoon light soy sauce

3.5 ounces (100 g) somen noodles

Juice of ½ lemon

3 scallions (green parts only), thinly sliced on the diagonal, for serving

(Tip:) The miso butter will keep in the refrigerator, well wrapped, for a few weeks.

Japanese-Style Udon Carbonara

Carbonara is an Italian dish made with spaghetti, but udon noodles go so well with a creamy sauce that I decided to use them instead. Note that this is not an authentic carbonara, but Japanese-style carbonara. Italian pasta dishes are popular in Japan, including spaghetti carbonara, but their way of preparing it is a bit different: They use heavy cream instead of cheeses such as Pecorino Romano and Parmesan, which aren't readily available in Japan. And adding miso gives it a Japanese flavor.

1 tablespoon vegetable oil or other neutral oil

1 garlic clove, minced

Half a 5-ounce (142 g) package plant-based bacon or one quarter of an 8-ounce (226 g) package smoked firm tofu, cut into short matchsticks

½ cup (120 ml) coconut cream

2 teaspoons white miso

1 teaspoon nutritional yeast, plus more for serving (optional)

8 ounces (227 g) frozen Homemade Udon Noodles (page 20) or store-bought udon (no need to thaw)

Salt and freshly ground black pepper

1. Heat the oil in a frying pan over medium heat. Add the garlic and plant-based bacon, and cook, stirring occasionally, until the plant-based bacon is deep golden brown. Remove from the heat.

2. To make the sauce, in a small bowl, combine the coconut cream, miso, and nutritional yeast. Stir well to combine.

3. Place the noodles in a deep microwave-safe bowl, cover, and microwave on high for 4 to 5 minutes, until hot and cooked through.

4. Add the sauce to the noodles. Mix well, and season with salt and pepper. Divide equally between two bowls.

5. Top with the plant-based bacon and garlic. Sprinkle with a little more nutritional yeast, if desired, and serve.

Kimchi Udon

This powerful trio of butter, kimchi, and gochujang is still by far my favorite combination, because the rich, intense flavor of the kimchi is the perfect complement to thick udon noodles. The butter makes the whole thing super creamy.

1. Melt the butter in a frying pan over low heat. Add the garlic, mushrooms, and kimchi, and cook for about 5 minutes. Add 2 tablespoons water, the soy sauce, gochugaru, and gochujang. Simmer for 2 to 3 minutes, until the sauce reduces a little.

2. Place the cooked noodles in a medium bowl. Pour over the kimchi sauce and mix well. Sprinkle with the sliced scallion and sesame seeds, and serve.

SERVES 1

- 3 tablespoons unsalted vegan butter
- 3 garlic cloves, minced
- 4 white button mushrooms, thinly sliced
- ¼ cup (37 g) coarsely chopped Chinese Cabbage Kimchi (page 14) or store-bought cabbage kimchi
- 1 tablespoon light soy sauce
- 1 tablespoon gochugaru (ground or flakes)
- 1 tablespoon gochujang
- 3.5 ounces (100 g) Homemade Udon Noodles (page 20) or store-bought fresh udon, cooked

GARNISH

- 1 scallion, 1 small leek (green parts only), or a few fresh chives, thinly sliced
- 1 teaspoon sesame seeds

Rabokki

Rabokki (라볶이) is the name for a mix of Korean instant ramen (ramyeon, 라면) and tteok bokki (Korean rice cakes). It's a very popular dish in Korea, especially among teenagers. It has a delicious and irresistible spicy flavor, and it's a filling meal for a relatively low price, which probably adds to its popularity.

1. Pour the vegetable dashi into a saucepan or wok and add the gochujang, gochugaru, soy sauce, and sugar. Mix well and bring to a boil over high heat. Add the garlic, scallions, and carrot. Bring back to a boil and cook for about 10 minutes, until the carrot is soft.

2. Add the rice cakes and the tofu (if using) to the broth and cook for 5 minutes. Add the noodles, turn down the heat to medium-low, and simmer gently for another 5 minutes, until all the noodles are cooked through.

3. Divide evenly between two bowls. Top each with half of the vegan cheese (if using). Sprinkle with the chopped scallion and sesame seeds, and serve.

SERVES 2

- 1⅔ cup (400 ml) Vegetable Dashi (page 12) or vegetable broth
- 2 tablespoons gochujang
- 1 tablespoon gochugaru (ground or flakes)
- 2 tablespoons light soy sauce
- 2 tablespoons superfine sugar
- 5 garlic cloves, minced
- 2 or 3 scallions, 1 small leek (white and green parts), or 1 small bunch fresh chives, coarsely chopped
- 1 carrot, peeled and grated
- 10 pieces Korean rice cake (tteok bokki)
- One quarter of a 14-ounce (397 g) block firm tofu, pressed and cubed (optional)
- Two 3-ounce (85 g) packages instant ramen noodles (reserve the flavoring packet for another use, if desired)

GARNISH

- 3.5 ounces (100 g) vegan cheese, grated or sliced (optional)
- 1 scallion, 1 small leek (white and green parts), or a few fresh chives, chopped
- 1 tablespoon sesame seeds

MORE NOODLE RECIPES

Superior Instant Noodles

Instant noodles are the ultimate lazy meal. On the rare occasion I eat them, I like to mix them with a flavorful spicy oil that I make in 5 minutes—once I've added the noodles, presto, I'm done! The result is a lightweight and spicy sauce that evenly coats the noodles and is absolutely delicious. These chile and garlic noodles have a perfectly balanced sweet, salty, tart, and lightly spicy flavor that will not numb your tongue!

1. Bring a pot of water to a boil and cook the noodles according to the package instructions until tender, about 2 minutes. Drain well.

2. In a heat-safe serving bowl, combine the garlic, gochugaru, brown sugar, soy sauce, vinegar, sesame seeds, and scallions. Stir well. Heat the oil in a small saucepan over high heat for about 1 minute, until barely smoking. Slowly pour it into the bowl. (The oil will sizzle—that's normal!) Stir to combine.

3. Add the noodles and mix well to coat them with the sauce. Sprinkle with the sliced scallions and sesame seeds, and serve hot.

SERVES 1

One 3-ounce (85 g) package instant ramen noodles (reserve the flavoring packet for another use, if desired)

3 tablespoons vegetable oil or other neutral oil

3 garlic cloves, minced

1 tablespoon gochugaru (ground or flakes)

1½ teaspoons brown sugar

2 tablespoons dark soy sauce

1 tablespoon rice vinegar

1 teaspoon sesame seeds

2 scallions, 1 small leek (white and green parts), or 1 small bunch fresh chives, chopped

GARNISH

3 scallions, 1 small leek (green parts only), or 1 small bunch fresh chives, thinly sliced

1 tablespoon sesame seeds

Noodles in Black Bean Sauce * JJAJANGMYEON

Jjajangmyeon (자장면), also called "zha jiang mian" in China, is a dish of noodles served with black bean sauce, which traditionally contains chunjang (a salty, dark soy paste), diced meat, and vegetables. It is a very popular dish of Sino-Korean origin. Sino-Korean cooking, also called "junghwa yori," was developed by the first Chinese immigrants to Korea. There are numerous theories about exactly when the dish originated in Korea. The first official jjajangmyeon is thought to come from a restaurant named Gonghwachun in the city of Incheon's Chinatown.

1. Heat ¾ cup (90 ml) of the oil in a small nonstick frying pan over medium heat. Add the black bean paste and stir until bubbles form. Remove from the heat.

2. In a wok, heat the remaining oil over medium heat. Add the mushrooms and cook, stirring occasionally, until they're golden brown. Add the sliced scallion. Stir until the scallion becomes fragrant. Add the ginger, garlic, and sugar. Stir, then add the onion, cabbage, and zucchini, and sauté until they begin to brown. Add the "oyster" sauce, soy sauce, and the fried black bean paste. Mix well.

3. Stir in the vegetable dashi and bring to a boil. Lower the heat and simmer for 10 minutes. Adjust salt to taste. Add the cornstarch slurry to the sauce, stirring in 1 teaspoon at a time, and cook until the sauce thickens. Remove from the heat.

4. Bring a pot of water to a boil and cook the noodles according to the package instructions until tender, 3 to 4 minutes. Drain, then rinse under cold water to prevent the noodles from cooking further, until they are cold to the touch. Drain well. Divide equally between two deep bowls.

5. To serve, move the noodles to one side of each bowl, and add half of the sauce to the other side. Top each bowl with the cucumber. Serve the pickled radish on the side. Mix the noodles and sauce well before eating, so every noodle is coated with sauce.

SERVES 2

- ¾ cup (90 ml) plus 3 tablespoons vegetable oil or other neutral oil
- 3 tablespoons black bean paste (chunjang)
- ½ pound (180 g) white button or shiitake mushrooms, stems removed, coarsely chopped
- 1 scallion, 1 small leek (white and green parts), or 1 small bunch fresh chives, thinly sliced
- ½ teaspoon minced fresh ginger
- 1 tablespoon minced garlic
- 2 tablespoons superfine sugar
- 1 onion, chopped
- 2 cabbage leaves, chopped
- ½ medium zucchini, coarsely chopped
- 1 tablespoon "Oyster" Sauce (page 18)
- 1 tablespoon dark soy sauce
- 2 cups (480 ml) Vegetable Dashi (page 12), vegetable broth, or water
- Salt (optional)
- 1 tablespoon cornstarch mixed with 1 tablespoon water to make a slurry
- 8 ounces (227 g) jjajangmyeon (thick wheat) noodles, thawed if frozen
- ½ English cucumber, cut into thin matchsticks
- One 2-inch (5 cm) piece yellow pickled radish (danmuji), thinly sliced (optional)

Crispy Noodles with Sautéed Vegetables * MÌ XÀO GIÒN

Mì xào giòn is one of my favorite dishes. Nothing compares to this ultra-crispy golden nest of noodles glazed in a rich garlic-soy sauce. I love to take a bite from the center of the nest, where the sauce has softened the noodles, and savor both soft and crunchy noodles at the same time. It's a true culinary masterpiece!

1. To make the sauce, in a small bowl, add the "oyster" sauce, light soy sauce, dark soy sauce, sugar, black pepper, and sesame oil. Stir to combine.

2. To fry the noodles, heat 2 cups (480 ml) of the oil in a deep saucepan or wok over medium heat. Set a wire rack over a rimmed baking sheet. Separate the noodles into two equal portions and shape them each into a bird's nest. Using a slotted spoon, carefully slip one noodle nest into the oil and cook for 10 to 20 seconds, until the noodles puff up and become crunchy. Flip the nest over and fry the other side for another 10 to 20 seconds. Using the slotted spoon, transfer the noodles to drain on the prepared wire rack. Repeat with the other nest.

3. Heat the remaining vegetable oil in a large saucepan over medium heat. Add the onion and garlic and cook, stirring occasionally, until golden and fragrant. Add the bell pepper, broccoli, mushrooms, bok choy, and carrot, and sauté for 2 to 3 minutes, until the vegetables are brown at the edges. Reserve 2 tablespoons of the sauce for serving, then stir the remaining sauce into the vegetables.

4. Add the vegetable dashi to the vegetables and bring to a boil. Add the cornstarch slurry to the broth, stirring in 1 teaspoon at a time, and cook for 30 seconds, until the broth thickens. Turn down the heat and simmer until the vegetables are tender.

5. To serve, place each noodle nest in a wide, shallow bowl. Use a slotted spoon to top each equally with the vegetables. Pour over the broth, and drizzle each with a tablespoon of the reserved sauce.

SERVES 2

SAUCE

- 2 tablespoons "Oyster" Sauce (page 18)
- 1 tablespoon light soy sauce
- 1 tablespoon dark soy sauce
- 1 tablespoon superfine sugar
- 1 teaspoon freshly ground black pepper
- 3 tablespoons toasted sesame oil

NOODLES AND VEGETABLES

- 2 cups (480 ml) plus 1 tablespoon vegetable oil or other neutral oil
- 8 ounces (227 g) fresh Chinese wheat (chow mein) noodles
- 1 small white onion, cut into matchsticks
- 1 garlic clove, minced
- 1 small green bell pepper, seeded and cut into matchsticks
- ½ broccoli, cut into florets
- 5 white button mushrooms, thinly sliced
- 1 small head bok choy, leaves separated
- 1 small carrot, peeled and cut into ½-inch-thick (1.25 cm) coins
- ½ cup (120 ml) plus 2 tablespoons Vegetable Dashi (page 12) or vegetable broth
- 2 tablespoons cornstarch mixed with 3 tablespoons water to make a slurry

Acknowledgments

Thanks goes to you, my friend Alie, photographer and second mother. You supported and encouraged me all the way through this project and helped me more than you know.

Thank you to my mom, who knew how to motivate me at all times and has always inspired me. You are my daily inspiration, and my passion for cooking comes from you.

Thank you to Lucie for your support.

Thank you to everyone who made this book possible— Céline, and the entire team at Éditions La Plage—a big thanks.

Thank you to all who buy this book and take the time to make these recipes with love and care.

And finally, I thank myself for making one of my dreams come true and proving to myself that I could do it.

INDEX

NOTE: Page numbers in *italics* indicate a photograph.

The Experiment, LLC
220 East 23rd Street, Suite 600
New York, NY 10010-4658
theexperimentpublishing.com

Library of Congress Cataloging-in-Publication Data available upon request

ISBN 978-1-891011-26-9
Ebook ISBN 978-1-891011-27-6

Cover and text design, and photographs on pages 2–3, by Beth Bugler
Photographs on pages 4–7 by Adobe Stock: Chan (kombu), rdnzl (nori),
Nikox2 (wakame), bellakadife (tahini), Bowonpat (gochujang),
Marina (miso), innafoto2017 (tofu), Cathleen (shiitake),
Elena Schweitzer (daikon)
Editorial direction by Céline Le Lamer
Translation by Lucinda Karter-Clements

Manufactured in China

First printing November 2023
10 9 8 7 6 5 4 3 2 1